The Monsters of Education Technology

AUDREY WATTERS

ISBN: 1505225051
ISBN-13: 978-1505225051

For Seymour

CONTENTS

INTRODUCTION

I was supposed to write a different book this year.

I do have several chapters of *Teaching Machines* written, I promise, and if you're one of the people who's told me how excited you are to read it, I'm sorry that it's taking me so long (but thank you for the continued encouragement).

I've done an incredible amount of research on the book – a cultural history of "teaching machines." I've fallen down a rabbit hole of patent history, for example, spending hours and hours looking at plans for the various devices that have claimed to automate teaching and learning. As a constant reminder to the project, my workspace is littered with books about the history of education technology, the work of B. F. Skinner and Sidney Pressey and Alan Kay and Seymour Papert and others. I bookmark any blog post about the latest developments in robot essay graders or the latest (re)discovery involving intelligent tutoring systems. Papers (yes, papers) and scribbled notes (yes, scribbled notes) pile up around me as I sit at my kitchen table... and work on other things.

Being a freelance writer is challenging in the best of times (and no, hyping a "freelance economy" does not make this "the best of times"); and in the last year or so, I've been supplementing that "Please Donate" button on the Hack Education website with a little public speaking.

With *a lot* of public speaking.

Over the course of 2014, I have delivered over 14 unique talks and keynotes (a number that doesn't include panels or workshops or webinars). Do please note that adjective there. "Unique."

Many on the "ed-tech speaking circuit" have told me that I'm doing it wrong. You're supposed to prepare one talk – one talk that is well honed and, of course, can be extended and/or localized. You tell the audience at every stop along the way that one thing; you repeat that one message that ostensibly you were hired to deliver. (Bonus points if the presentation is already available via a TED Talk, and they still asked you to perform in person.)

Instead, I wrote a bunch of new stuff and tried to work through various ideas. I did so because I am both furious and curious about education technology's past, present, and future. Certainly there was some overlap in these talks. In some cases, I repeated words and references and phrases and (gasp!) paragraphs. A lot of the ideas and arguments are, not surprisingly, connected.

I didn't give one talk again and again and again. And in not doing so, it appears that I actually produced a book, one that I wrote and read aloud in hour-long chunks to audiences across the US, Canada, and the UK. I spent 2014 on a book tour for a book I hadn't yet written.

Each chapter here was written to be delivered orally. As such, some of these veer towards sermons and exhortations; they were written to stand on their own. I have made a few edits, tightened some language, cut some banter, and added a poorly formatted bibliography. The "original" versions are available on Hack Education, where you can also find links to slides, video, and audio.

The first section of the book explores the "hidden" history of education technology. Hidden or lost or purposefully ignored. In these talks, I tried to unearth and retell the stories of early education technologists, always asking why it is that ed-tech today operates with such a vigorous denial of its past.

The second section examines the ideology (ideologies) of ed-tech. Much like its history, this is something we all too often fail to grapple with, even though I hope we'd agree that neither education nor technology are ever ideology-free.

The final section alludes to the talk from which the title of this book is drawn: "Ed-Tech's Monsters." I delivered a keynote by that name at the Association for Learning Technology conference in September. It is in this final section of the book that I try to be optimistic.

Or at least I try to point out what an important moment we find ourselves: a moment where education technology is poised to either become more monstrous or more marvelous.

I am hopeful that in 2015, I'll be able to finish *Teaching Machines*. In the meantime, thank you for reading and supporting my work throughout 2014.

I. THE HIDDEN HISTORY OF ED-TECH

1 THE HISTORY OF THE FUTURE OF ED-TECH

A couple of months ago, my brother Fred and I went back to the house we grew up in. We're getting to the age where we have parents that are "that age." Our dad had fallen, broken his hip, and was in a nursing home. We went to his house to "check on things."

It's been over 20 years since either of us lived there. My bedroom has since become the guest bedroom. With the exception of the old bookshelf and bed, there's nothing there that's "me." But my brother's room has become a shrine to the Fred that was. It remains almost entirely untouched since he graduated from high school and moved out to attend the Air Force Academy. It's pretty weird to visit the room now. Fred didn't stay in the Air Force Academy. He dropped out after his sophomore year, became an environmental activist and then an emergency room nurse; he's now a nurse practitioner in Maine.

Visiting his old bedroom was like stepping into the past that felt strangely disconnected from the present. Not totally disconnected; strangely disconnected. You could find glimpses there of the kid he was, of the person he was supposed to become – of my parents' and grandparents' visions of and plans for his future.

A future predicted in the 1970s and 1980s.

It's not the future that came to be. The room contained the history of that not-future.

We found on his bookshelf another example of this: *The Kids' Whole Future Catalog*. Published in 1982, I remember how Fred and I would pour over this book. My brother admitted that it had shaped his thoughts at the time on who he would become, his expectations of what his future would look like.

It's a future of food factories and space vacations and flying trains. It's a future where robots are teachers.

Again, like my little brother's room, it's mostly the future that wasn't. Or the future that isn't quite. Or the future that isn't quite yet.

I want to talk about the history of the future of education technology this morning. The future that wasn't. The future that isn't quite. The future that isn't quite yet. The history of all of this.

I want us to consider where education technology has come from, where we have been. As educators. As technologists. Where are we going? What narratives help us answer questions about the past? What narratives help us shape the future?

As we move forward into a world that it increasingly governed by machines and algorithms, I think we must consider the trajectory of the path we're on. Because "the future of ed-tech" is shaped by the history of ed-tech – whether we realize it or not.

Last year, the programmer and designer Bret Victor delivered what I thought was one of the smartest keynotes I've ever seen.

He came on stage dressed in a button-up shirt and tie with pocket protector and proceeded to utilize an overhead projector and transparencies for his talk. There are three visual cues there about the conceit of his talk: the pocket protector, the overhead projector, and transparencies.

Victor spoke about the future of programming, but as those visual cues and those presentation technologies implied, he spoke of the future as though he was describing it in 1973. "Given what we know now," he asked, "what might programming be like 40 years from now?" In other words, given what we knew about computing in 1973, what would it be like in 2013?

Victor proceeded to talk about some of the computer science research that had been conducted in the previous decade – that is, in the 1960s. This was the research that he used to inform his predictions about the future:

Gordon Moore, Intel's co-founder for example, postulated in 1965 what we now call "Moore's Law," the observation that over the history of computing hardware, the number of transistors on integrated circuits doubles approximately every two years. In other words, the processing power of computer chips doubles roughly every two years. This is a prediction that has come true, but in part because the technology sector was worked to make this a self-fulfilling prophesy of sorts. Chip manufacturers like Intel have made increased computing power year-over-year an explicit goal.

But much of the research that Bret Victor cites in his keynote was never really adopted by the technology industry. It simply wasn't the focus. It wasn't the goal. Victor points to a number of incredibly interesting and provocative research efforts that went nowhere.

The Future of Programming that wasn't.

And it isn't that these innovative ideas were rejected or ignored because they just weren't do-able. What's worse, they *were* do-able, but they were ignored and forgotten. The technology that powers our computing systems today took a very different path than the one that Victor wryly describes in his talk. And today, many programmers don't recognize, let alone teach others, that there could be other ways of doing things, of designing and developing technologies.

Take the work of Douglas Englebart, for example. He passed away last year, an amazing but largely unsung visionary in computer science. Among other things, Englebart was the first to use an external device that rolled around on a flat surface and moved a pointer on a screen so as to highlight text and to select options – what we now call the mouse.

Englebart unveiled the mouse in what technologists refer fondly to as "The Mother of All Demos," a demonstration in 1968 of the oN-Line System (more commonly known as NLS), a hardware and software package that had a number of incredible features demonstrated publicly for the first time. Again, remember, this was the era of the mainframe and the punch-card. In the demo: the mouse, "windows," hypertext, graphics, version control, word processing, video conferencing, and a collaborative real-time editor.

1968.

But many of the features in "the Mother of All Demos" weren't picked up by the tech industry – at least, not right away. The team that had worked with Englebart on the NLS soon dispersed from their Stanford University-based research program, many of them ending up at Xerox PARC (Xerox's Palo Alto Research Center). In turn Xerox PARC became the site where many more of the computing technologies we do now take for granted were developed, including the Ethernet, laser printing, and the personal computer as we know it today.

But even at Xerox PARC, new technologies were devised that were never widely adopted. Why? Why, when as Victor argues, many of these were more interesting and elegant solutions than what we have actually ended up with?

In part, it's because computing technologies can be prototyped quite readily. The 1960s and 1970s marked the beginning of this: computers had become powerful enough to do interesting things, and many computer scientists were busily imagining what those interesting things might be and how they might be done. But while building new technologies is easy (or easy-ish), changing behaviors and culture is much, much harder.

What does this have to do with ed-tech?

Well, the tension between new tools and old practices should give you a hint. It's simple to introduce iPads into the classroom, for example. It's much more difficult to use them to do entirely new things, particularly things that run counter to how classrooms have operated in the past.

Watching Victor's talk, I couldn't help but wonder how might we have written "The Future of Ed-Tech" in the 1970s. After all, Bret Victor says that his keynote was inspired by Alan Kay, an important figure not just in programming but in education technology as well.

Kay was a pioneer in object-oriented programming. He actually attended Englebart's demo in 1968, and he later worked at Xerox PARC where he helped develop the programming language SmallTalk. (MIT Media Lab's introductory programming language for kids, Scratch, is based in part on SmallTalk.) And Alan Kay designed the prototype for something called the DynaBook, "a personal computer for children of all ages."

If I were to tell you the story, using the conceit that Bret Victor used in his keynote – that is, if I were to come out here today and tell you about the future of education technology as it might have been seen in the early 1970s – I would ground the talk in Alan Kay's DynaBook.

Again, let's recall that in the late Sixties and early Seventies, computers were still mostly giant mainframes, and even the growing market for microcomputers was largely restricted to scientists and the military. Alan Kay was among those instrumental in pushing forward a vision of personal computing.

We scoff now at the IBM CEO who purportedly said, "I think there is a world market for maybe five computers." But "personal computing" for Kay wasn't simply that computers would be adopted in the workplace. That's something you can imagine that every IBM executive would readily agree to.

Kay argued that computers should be commonplace and be used by millions of non-professional users. Kay believed this would foster a new literacy, one that would change the world much like the printing press did in the 16th and 17th century. And key: children would be the primary actors in this transformation.

In 1972 Kay published a manifesto, "A Personal Computer for Children of All Ages," in which he describes the DynaBook, the underlying vision as well as its technical specifications: no larger than a notebook, weighing less than four pounds, connected to a network, and all for a price tag of $500, which Kay explains at length is "not totally outrageous." ($500 was roughly the cost at the time of a color TV.)

"What then is a personal computer?" Kay writes. "One would hope that it would be both a medium for containing and expressing arbitrary symbolic notations, and also a collection of useful tools for manipulating these structures, with ways to add new tools to the repertoire." That is, it is a computer program but one that is completely programmable.

"It is now within the reach of current technology to give all the Beths and their dads a 'DynaBook' to use anytime, anywhere as they may wish," Kay writes in his 1972 manifesto. 1972 – 40 years before the iPad. "Although it can be used to communicate with others through the 'knowledge utilities' of the future such as a school 'library' (or business information system), we think that a large fraction of its use will involve reflexive communication of the owner with himself through this personal medium, much as paper and notebooks are currently used." The personal computer isn't "personal" because it's small and portable and yours to own. It's "personal" because you pour yourself into it – your thoughts, your programming.

So, if I were to tell you a story about the future of ed-tech like Bret Victor tells about the future of programming, I'd probably start from there, from the DynaBook's design in 1972. And it would be a story, like Victor's, with a subtext of sadness and loss that this is not what history has given us at all.

In some ways, the DynaBook does look a lot like our modern-day tablet computers. It looks a lot like the iPad even. (Kay did work at Apple, I should note, in the 1980s under then CEO John Scully). But as Kay has said in recent interviews, the iPad is not the actualization of the DynaBook.

He told *TIME* magazine last year that the primary purpose of the DynaBook was "to simulate all existing media in an editable/authorable form in a highly portable networked (including wireless) form. The main point was for it to be able to qualitatively extend the notions of 'reading, writing, sharing, publishing, etc. of ideas' literacy to include the 'computer reading, writing, sharing, publishing of ideas' that is the computer's special province. For all media, the original intent was 'symmetric authoring and consuming'."

Consumption and creation: that's a tension that's plagued the iPads since they were unveiled. But it's one that the DynaBook was designed to balance.

"Isn't it crystal clear," Kay continued in his *TIME* interview, "that this last and most important service [authoring and consuming] is quite lacking in today's computing for the general public? Apple with the iPad and iPhone goes even further and does not allow children to download an Etoy made by another child somewhere in the world. This could not be farther from the original intentions of the entire ARPA-IPTO/PARC community in the '60s and '70s."

For Kay, the DynaBook was meant to help build capacity so that children (and adults too) would create their own interactive learning tools. The DynaBook was not simply about a new piece of hardware or new software, but about a new literacy, a new way of teaching and learning. And that remains largely unrealized.

Again, as Bret Victor's talk reminds us: changing technology is easy; changing practices, not so much.

Alan Kay's work draws heavily on that of Seymour Papert. (Bret Victor's work does too, I should add. As does mine.) Kay cites one of Papert's best-known lines in his manifesto: "should the computer program the kid or should the kid program the computer?"

Kay's work and Papert's work insist on the latter.

Kay met Papert in 1968 and learned then of Papert's work on the Logo programming language.

As a programming language, Logo not only helped teach children programming concepts but also helped develop their "body-syntonic reasoning." That is, Logo – and particularly the Turtle that the language became most synonymous with – helped give students an embodied understanding of mathematics. There was a Turtle robot and later a Turtle graphic on the screen. Using Logo, students could manipulate these; and this, Papert argued, would help them to understand and reason mathematically.

Computers, argued Papert, should unlock children's "powerful ideas." That's the subtitle to his 1980 book *Mindstorms*, a book that both Bret Victor and I insist you read. The book addresses "how computers can be carriers of powerful ideas and of the seeds of cultural change, how they can help people form new relationships with knowledge that cut across the traditional lines separating humanities from sciences and knowledge of the self from both of these. It is about using computers to challenge current beliefs about who can understand what and at what age. It is about using computers to question standard assumptions in developmental psychology and in the psychology of aptitudes and attitudes. It is about whether personal computers and the cultures in which they are used will continue to be the creatures of 'engineers' alone or whether we can construct intellectual environments in which people who today think of themselves as 'humanists' will feel part of, not alienated from, the process of constructing computational cultures."

Computers, Papert insisted, will help children gain "a sense of mastery over a piece of the most modern and powerful technology and establish an intimate contact with some of the deepest ideas from science, from mathematics, and from the art of intellectual model building."

Mindstorms. 1980.

Yet sadly Papert's work might be another example of the "Future of Ed-Tech" that hasn't come to pass. He does address this in part in his 1993 book *The Children's Machine*: "Progressive teachers knew very well how to use the computer for their own ends as an instrument of change; School knew very well how to nip this subversion in the bud."

As Bret Victor argues in his keynote: developing new technologies is easy; changing human behaviors, changing institutions, challenging tradition and power is hard.

"Computer-aided inspiration" as Papert envisioned has been mostly trumped by "computer-aided instruction."

Indeed, computer-aided instruction came under development around the same time as Logo and the DynaBook – even earlier, actually. And the history of the future of computer-aided instruction may well tell us more about the ed-tech we've inherited. It certainly points to the ed-tech that many people still want us to have.

The first computer-aided instruction system was PLATO (short for Programmed Logic for Automatic Teaching Operations), a computer system developed at the University of Illinois. 1960 saw the first version, the PLATO I, operate on the university's ILLIAC I computer. Then came PLATO II, PLATO III, and PLATO IV.

The PLATO IV was released in 1972, the same year as Alan Kay's manifesto. It's roughly the same time as Bret Victor situates his "Future of Programming" keynote.

Early versions of the PLATO system had a student terminal attached to a mainframe. The software offered mostly "drill and kill" and tutorial lessons. But as the PLATO system developed, new and more sophisticated software was added – more problem-based and inquiry-based lessons, for example. A new programming language called TUTOR enabled "anyone" to create their own PLATO lessons without having to be a programmer. The mainframe now supported multiple, networked computers. Students could communicate with one another, in addition to the instructor. Pretty groundbreaking stuff as this was all pre-Internet.

This networked system made PLATO the site for a number of very important innovations in computing technology, not to mention in ed-tech. Forums, message boards, chat rooms, instant messaging, screen sharing, multiplayer games, and emoticons. PLATO was, as author Brian Dear argues in his forthcoming book *The Friendly Orange Glow* "the dawn of cyberculture."

And again, the familiar story: PLATO's contribution to cyberculture is mostly forgotten.

Arguably PLATO's contribution to ed-tech has been forgotten as well. I'm not sure. I think that we can see in PLATO many of the features in ed-tech today, many of the features that would make Alan Kay and Seymour Papert shudder.

One of the features PLATO boasted: tracking every keystroke that a student made, data on every answer submitted, right or wrong. PLATO offered more efficient computer-based testing. It offered the broadcast of computer-based lessons to multiple locations, where students could work at their own pace. Indeed, by the mid-Seventies, PLATO was serving students in over 150 locations – not just across the University of Illinois campus, but also in elementary schools, high schools, and on military bases.

Sensing a huge business opportunity, the Control Data Corporation, the company that built the University of Illinois mainframe, announced that it was going to go to market with PLATO, spinning it out from a university project to a corporate one.

This is where that $500 price tag for Alan Kay's DynaBook is so significant.

CDC charged $50 an hour for access to its mainframe, for starters. Each student unit cost about $1900; the mainframe itself cost at least $2.5 million, according to estimates in a 1973 review of computer-assisted instruction. CDC charged $300,000 to develop each piece of courseware.

Needless to say, PLATO as a computer-aided instruction product was a failure. The main success that CDC had with it: selling an online testing system to the National Association of Securities Dealers, a regulatory group that licenses people who sell securities. CDC sold the PLATO trademark in 1989 to The Roach Organization, and it now sells e-learning software under the name Edmentum.

From a machine at "the dawn of cyberculture" to one that delivered standardized testing for stockbrokers. The history of the future of ed-tech. The refrain of this talk: new technologies are easy to develop; new behaviors and new cultures are not.

One final piece of education technology history, this one a little older than the computer-based innovations of the 1960s and 1970s. It's still a machine-based innovation. It's still an object that enables efficient instruction and efficient assessment.

B. F. Skinner's "teaching machine."

I could go back farther than Skinner, admittedly. To a patent in 1866 for a device to teach spelling. Or to a patent in 1909 for a device to teach reading. Or to a patent in 1911 awarded to one Herbert Aikens that promised to teach "arithmetic, reading, spelling, foreign languages, history, geography, literature or any other subject in which questions can be asked in such a way as to demand a definite form of words ... letters ... or symbols."

I could go back to the machine developed by Sidney Pressey. Pressey was psychologist at Ohio State University, and he came up with an idea for a machine to score the intelligence tests that the military was using to determine eligibility to enlistment. Then World War I happened, causing a delay in Pressey's work. He first exhibited his teaching machine at the 1925 meeting of the American Psychological Association. It had four multiple-choice questions and answers in a window, and four keys. If the student thought the second answer was correct, she pressed the second key; if she was right, the next question was turned up. If the second was not the right answer, the initial question remained in the window, and the student persisted until she found the right one. A record of all the student's attempts was kept automatically.

Intelligence testing based on students' responses to multiple-choice questions. Multiple-choice questions with four answers. Sound familiar?

Harvard professor B. F. Skinner claimed he'd never seen Pressey's device when he developed his own teaching machine in the mid 1950s. Indeed, he dismissed Pressey's device, arguing it was a *testing* and not a *teaching* machine. Skinner didn't like that Pressey's machine featured multiple-choice questions. His enabled students to enter their own responses by pulling a series of levers. The correct answer made a light go on.

A behaviorist, Skinner believed that teaching machines could provide an ideal mechanism for operant conditioning. "There is no reason why the schoolroom should be any less mechanized than, for example, the kitchen," he argued.

Skinner believed that immediate, positive reinforcement was key to shaping behavior. All human actions could be analyzed this way. Skinner contended that, despite their important role in helping to shape student behavior, "the simple fact is that, as a mere reinforcing mechanism, the teacher is out of date."

Skinner's teaching machine might look terribly out-of-date, but I'd argue that *this* is the history that still shapes so much of what we see today. Self-paced learning, gamification, an emphasis on real-time or near-real-time corrections. No doubt, ed-tech today draws quite heavily on Skinner's ideas because Skinner (and his fellow education psychologist Edward Thorndike) has been so influential in how we view teaching and learning and how we view schooling.

So much B. F. Skinner. So little Seymour Papert. So little Alan Kay.

I'd argue too that this isn't just about education technology. There's so much Skinner and so little Kay in "mainstream" technology too. Think Zynga, for example. Click, click, click. Level up! Rewards! Achievement unlocked!

As we see our society becoming more and more "technological," it's worth considering the origins and the trajectory of all that tech.

I'll quote Papert here, one more time, to close: "One might say the computer is being used to program the child. In my vision, the child programs the computer, and in doing so, both acquires a sense of mastery over a piece of the most modern and powerful technology and establishes an intense contact with some of the deepest ideas from science, from mathematics, and from the art of intellectual model building."

May that vision be what guides us forward. May that be what shapes the future of ed-tech.

This keynote was delivered on February 4, 2014 at the EdTechTeacher iPad Summit in San Diego, California. The original version can be found on Hack Education at http://hackeducation.com/2014/02/04/the-history-of-the-future-of-ed-tech/

WORKS CITED

Brian Dear, *The Friendly Orange Glow: The Story of the PLATO System and the Dawn of Cyberculture.* http://friendlyorangeglow.com/

David Greelish, "An Interview with Computing Pioneer Alan Kay." *TIME.* April 2, 2013. http://techland.time.com/2013/04/02/an-interview-with-computing-pioneer-alan-kay/

Alan Kay, "A Personal Computer for Children of All Ages." Proceedings of the ACM Annual Conference. 1971. Vol 1, No. 1.

Seymour Papert, *The Children's Machine: Rethinking School in the Age of the Computer.* Basic Books. 1993.

Seymour Papert, *Mindstorms: Children, Computers, and Powerful Ideas.* Basic Books. 1980.

B. F. Skinner, *The Technology of Teaching.* Copley Publishing Group. 1968.

Paula Taylor, *The Kids' Whole Future Catalog.* Random House Books for Young Readers. 1982.

Bret Victor, "The Future of Programming," Dropbox's DBX Conference. July 9, 2013. http://vimeo.com/71278954

2 UN-FATHOMABLE: THE HIDDEN HISTORY OF ED-TECH

A couple of years ago, a friend sent me an exasperated email on the heels of an exclusive technology event he'd attended in Northern California – not in Silicon Valley, but close enough – one with powerful people in the tech industry. Investors. Engineers. Entrepreneurs. Several prominent CEOs of prominent ed-tech startups had been invited to speak there about the state of education – past, present, and future – and their talks, my friend reported, tended to condemn education's utter failure to change or to adopt computing technologies. The personal computing revolution had passed schools by entirely, they argued, and it wasn't until the last decade that schools had started to even consider the existence of the Internet. The first online class, insisted one co-founder of a company that's raised tens of millions of dollars in venture capital since then, was in 2001 at MIT.

And okay, in fairness, these folks are not historians. They're computer scientists, artificial intelligence experts, software engineers. They're entrepreneurs. But their lack of knowledge about the history of education and the history of education technology matters.

It matters because it supports a prevailing narrative about innovation – *where* innovation comes from (according to this narrative, it comes from private industry, and not from public institutions; from Silicon Valley, that is, not from elsewhere in the world) and *when* it comes (there's this fiercely myopic fixation on the future).

The lack of knowledge about history matters too because it reflects and even enables a powerful strain in American ideology and in the ideology of the technology industry: that the past is irrelevant, that the past is a monolithic block of brokenness – unchanged and unchanging until it's disrupted by technological innovation, or by the promise of technological

12

innovation, by the future itself.

This ideology shapes the story that many ed-tech entrepreneurs tell about education and about their role in transforming it.

One of my favorite examples of this comes from Salman Khan, the founder of Khan Academy, in a video on "The History of Education" he made with *Forbes* writer Michael Noer in 2012.

It's the history of education "from 1680 to 2050" told in 11 minutes, so needless to say it's a rather abbreviated version of events. It's not titled "The History of Education in the United States," although that would be much better because contributions to education from the rest of the world are entirely absent.

Well, except for the Prussians. Americans involved in education reform and education technology love to talk about the Prussians.

Our current model of education, says Khan, originated at the turn of the nineteenth century: "age-based cohorts" that move through an "assembly line" with "information being delivered at every point."

"This is the Prussian model," the *Forbes* writer Noer adds, "and it's about as inflexible as a Prussian can be." But Khan notes that there were benefits to this as "it was the first time people said, 'No, we want everyone to get an education for free.'"

Then "Horace Mann comes along about 1840" and introduces this concept of free education for everyone to the United States. By 1870, says Khan, public education is pretty common "but even at that point it wasn't uniform" with different standards and curriculum in different states and cities. So in 1892, "something that tends to get lost in history," a committee of ten – "somewhat Orwellian" quips Noer – meet to determine what twelve years of compulsory public education should look like.

"It was forward looking for 120 years ago," says Noer, "but what's interesting is that we've basically been stuck there for 120 years." Education has been "static to the present day," agrees Khan.

And from 1892, the story they tell jumps ahead, straight to the invention of the Internet – "the mid late Nineties," says Khan as he plots it on his timeline. "The big thing here," says Noer as the two skip over one hundred years or so of history, "is what you've done" with Khan Academy. "One person with one computer can reach millions." This revolutionizes lectures, Noer argues; it revolutionizes homework. "Class time is liberated," adds Khan. This changes everything. Khan Academy (founded in 2006) changes everything that has been stagnant and static since the nineteenth century.

See, this isn't simply a matter of forgetting history – the history of technology or the history of education or the history of ed-tech. It's not simply a matter of ignoring it. It's a rewriting of history, whether you see it as activist or accidental.

To contend, as my friend overheard at that tech event or as Khan implies in his history of education, that schools haven't been involved in the development or deployment of computers or the Internet, for example, is laughably incorrect. It's an inaccurate, incomplete history of computing technology, not simply an inaccurate history of ed-tech.

Take the ILLIAC I, the first von Neumann architecture computer owned by an American university, built in 1952 at the University of Illinois. (The US was beaten by several years by universities here in the UK, I should point out, namely at the nearby University of Manchester.)

Or take PLATO, a computer-based education system, sometimes credited as the first piece of educational computing software, built on the University of Illinois' ILLIAC machine in 1960.

Or take the work of Marc Andreessen, now a powerful figure in Silicon Valley, a venture capitalist with several major investments in ed-tech, who took the work he'd done on the Mosaic Web browser as a student at the University of Illinois in order to start his own company, Mosaic Communications Company, which eventually became the Netscape Communications Company, launching the Netscape Navigator web browser and successfully IPOing in 1995.

The history of education technology is long. The history of education technology is rich. And while it certainly predates Netscape or the von Neumann architecture, the history of education technology is deeply intertwined with the history of computing – and visa versa.

And I could probably stop right there with my keynote. This is really the crux of my message: there's a fascinating and important history of education technology that is largely forgotten, that is largely hidden. It's overlooked for a number of reasons, some of which is wrapped up in the ideologies I've already alluded to.

All this means, if we're going to talk about "Building the Digital Institution: Technological Innovation in Universities and Colleges," the theme of this conference, we probably should know a bit about the history of universities and colleges and technological innovation and build from there.

Despite all the problems that these institutions have – and good grief, they do have problems – universities and colleges *have been* the sites of technological innovation. They *are* the sites of technological innovation. Or they can be. In pockets, to be sure. In spurts, to be sure. Certain developments in certain times in certain places, yes. Certain disciplines making breakthroughs; certain disciplines getting the credit. Certain universities getting the credit for innovating, even when, dare I say, they aren't actually doing anything that new or transformative.

It's not surprising perhaps that the ed-tech startup co-founder in my opening anecdote would credit MIT with offering the first online course. It's one of those universities that consistently gets the credit for "innovation." Perhaps he was thinking of MIT OpenCourseWare which launched in 2002 as an effort to put the university's course materials online in a free and openly licensed format.

A couple of side-notes: 1) That putting course materials online could be confused with offering a course online speaks volumes about this co-founder's startup. 2) This particular ed-tech co-founder attended MIT. 3) Salman Khan is also a MIT graduate, and I think his vision for teaching and learning via a site like Khan Academy draws heavily on that MIT academic culture, where class attendance isn't as important as working through course materials at your own pace with your smartest peers. As long as you can pass the assessments at the end of the course, that's what matters.

It's unlikely, when touting who put classes online first that this ed-tech co-founder from my opening anecdote was thinking of Fathom, the Columbia University-led online learning initiative founded roughly around the date he ascribed to the first "online course." It's unlikely he was thinking of AllLearn, the Stanford, Yale, and Oxford Universities-led online learning initiative of the same period.

Possibly because it's like the movie *Fight Club*. The first rule of the history of online education: you don't talk about Fathom. You don't talk about AllLearn.

And this particular ed-tech startup co-founder certainly wasn't talking about UK e-University, because as with the development of early computers, we ("we Americans," I should qualify here) seem to have forgotten that much has happened outside of the US, let alone outside of Silicon Valley.

Ah, ed-tech of the late 1990s and early 2000s. "The Internet!" as Salman Khan exclaims excitedly.

We don't talk much about that period. We don't talk much about the heady days of the first Dot Com bubble. Have we really forgotten?

It could be that we're reluctant in talking about the first Dot Com bubble because some of us don't want to admit we might just be in the midst of another one. Startups, ed-tech and otherwise, are overhyped and overfunded and overvalued, many with little to show in terms of profit (or educational outcomes).

What's implied by our silence about the Dot Com era perhaps: we know better now than we did then. Or at least the tech is better. Or at least we're not spending as much money to launch startups these days. Or we care more about learning now. Or something.

And yes, some of us simply don't want to talk about the tech and ed-tech failures of the Dot Com era – the failures of Fathom and AllLearn and UKeU and the like – because of the shame of failure. It's not just Silicon Valley entrepreneurs who are at fault here. I think industry and institutions (particularly elite Ivy League institutions) have buried those failures. That's a pity since there's much to learn.

I realize that most of the folks here know these stories, but I'm going to repeat them anyway.

Fathom opened in 2000 and closed in 2003.

AllLearn opened in 2001 and closed in 2006.

UKeU opened in 2003 and closed in 2004.

$30 million invested into the Fathom initiative by Columbia University.

$12 million was invested into AllLearn from various schools and foundations.

£62 million was earmarked for and £50 million was spent by the British government on UKeU.

For a little comparison: edX launched in 2012 with an initial $60 million investment from Harvard and (yes) MIT. Coursera launched in 2012 with a total venture capital investment of $85 million. Udacity launched in 2012 with a total (disclosed) venture capital investment of $20 million.

This notion that it's easier and cheaper to launch a startup in the 2010s, that thanks to open source technologies and the cloud and the like that we needn't funnel so much money into ed-tech startups. Well...

Thanks to the Internet Archive Wayback Machine, we can see what Fathom and AllLearn's websites looked like circa 2001. It's an important tool as if you search for "UKeU" today, you might accidentally stumble upon Ukulele University. If you compare these sites to contemporary online education sites like Coursera or FutureLearn, you can see some changes – improvements no doubt – in Web design. But what's really changed in the decade or so between the Dot Com-era online courses and today's versions? What's changed in terms of institutional involvement? What's changed in terms of branding? What's changed in terms of course content, and what's changed in terms of the "ed-tech" under the hood? What hasn't changed? What's the same?

The course content for Fathom and AllLearn was similar to what we see being offered online today. That's not a surprise, as such is the makeup of the typical college course catalog: a broad swath of classes in science, technology, humanities, professional development, business, and law. Some 2000 courses were offered via Fathom. There were 110 offered on AllLearn. 25 on UK e-University. (Is that correct?!) There are over 500 courses offered via Coursera.

The technology hasn't changed much in the intervening decade. (And the phrase "content delivery system" is still used to describe online education, sadly.) The Dot Com era courses offered "primary source documents, animations, interactive graphics, audio slide shows, and streaming videos." Today's online courses look much the same, and despite their boasts about better assessment tools – automated essay graders and the like – multiple choice quizzes, a historical artifact from the earliest teaching machines of the 20th century, still dominate.

The marketing pitch to students hasn't changed much either: "Online courses from the world's best universities" – that's the tagline on the edX site. The "world's best courses" – that's what Coursera promises. "Enjoy free online courses from leading UK and international universities" – that's FutureLearn's promise. The "world's most trusted sources of knowledge" – that was Fathom's. The focus, then and now, is on the prestige of the institutions involved. And they are some of the very same institutions. Stanford. Yale. Columbia.

AllLearn, short for the Alliance for Lifelong Learning, stressed that its classes were just that: an opportunity for continuing education and lifelong learning. Udacity stresses something different today: it's about "advancing your career." It's about "dream jobs."

There's been plenty of hype about these new online platforms displacing or replacing face-to-face education, and part of that does connect to another powerful (political) narrative: that universities do not adequately equip students with "21st century skills" that employers will increasingly demand. But by most accounts, those who sign up for these courses still fall into the "lifelong learner" category. The majority has a college degree already.

The question remains unresolved, a decade later, as to whether or not people will *pay* for these online courses (or for certification after successful completion) to such an extent that these online initiatives can ever become financially sustainable, let alone profitable. That's even accounting for the massive increase since the early 2000s in the cost of higher education (in the US and now elsewhere) alongside the growing demand for everyone to have some sort of college credential.

From a 2002 *New York Times* article about universities' efforts to move online, "Lessons Learned at Dot Com U": "college campuses and dot-coms had looked at the numbers and anticipated a rising tide of enrollment based on baby boomers and their children as both traditional students and those seeking continuing education. In short, the colleges essentially assumed that if they built it, students would come."

"We hope it's enough money to get us to profitability,'" Coursera co-founder Daphne Koller told *The New York Times* in the summer of 2013 when her company announced it had raised another $43 million. "We haven't really focused yet on when that might be." Echoing the *Field of Dreams* reference from a decade earlier – that's a baseball movie reference, a terrible thing to invoke in a keynote in the UK, I realize: if you build it, they will come. Indeed, Koller has admitted that her investors have told her that if you do the "right thing" in education, the profits will follow.

Perhaps they will.

We can see already the pressures for Coursera to find a path to profitability. It has raised $85 million in venture capital after all, not in university endowment or in foundation funding. In recent months, Coursera has shuffled its executive team quite a bit, adding a venture capitalist from fabled investment firm Kleiner Perkins Caufield and Byers as President and adding a former Yale President as CEO. Co-founder Andrew Ng has stepped away from day-to-day work at the company, although he remains Chairman of the Board.

The new CEO of Coursera, Richard Levin, as it just so happens, was at the helm at Yale in the AllLearn era. (He was the chair of AllLearn as well.) One might assume then that he must have a significant amount of expertise and much wisdom gleaned from the university's Dot Com era ed-tech ventures. Levin, an economist by training, must know a bit about the history of education and the history of technology and the history of ed-tech. Or at least he should know a bit about the history of the economics of ed-tech. Right?

In an interview with *The New York Times* this spring, Levin offered this explanation as to why AllLearn did not succeed: "It was too early. Bandwidth wasn't adequate to support the video. But we gained a lot of experience of how to create courses, and then we used it starting in 2007 to create very high quality videos, now supported by adequate bandwidth in many parts of the world, with the Open Yale courses. We've released over 40 of them, and they gained a wide audience."

AllLearn failed, he argues, because of bandwidth. Bandwidth.

"The Internet bandwidth in most homes was inadequate for properly sharing course material," Levin contends. Actually, AllLearn offered its materials via CD-ROM as well, and like many sites in that period, AllLearn recognized that streaming video content might be challenging for many users. It allowed them to turn off some of the high-bandwidth features and download rather than watch video online.

Remember too, AllLearn was marketed as a "lifelong learning" site. Its pitch was to alumni of the elite universities involved as well as to the general public. The former would pay about $200 per course; the latter about $250. (One creative writing class charged $800 in tuition.) So are we to believe that those groups – alumni and keen lifelong learners – were unable to access AllLearn due to bandwidth issues? That they'd balk at paying for good Internet but not balk at the AllLearn fees? This is an assertion, an explanation that my colleague Mike Caulfield has questioned:

"All-Learn folded in 2006, when broadband was at a meager 20% adoption. Today, it's different, supposedly. It's at 28%. Are we to really believe that somewhere in that 8% of the population is the difference between success and failure?" asks Caulfield.

Caulfield also questions what Levin learned from OpenYale, the ed-tech venture that followed the demise of AllLearn. By Caulfield's calculations, those courses were created using "$4 million dollars of Hewlett money. And the videos are basically recordings of class lectures. Four million dollars for forty filmed courses, or, if you prefer, $100,000 a course for video lectures."

That's close to the cost for course production you hear bandied about today by professors who've created Coursera classes, for what it's worth.

It's this discrepancy between the costs and the revenue, an inability to find a sustainable business model that plagued the Dot Com era online initiatives. From a 2003 article in the Columbia student newspaper: "Fathom spent money at an unsustainable rate. In 2001, Fathom burned through almost $15 million, and generated revenues of only $700,000." And this is what plagues Coursera today.

This is (in part) why history matters. Well, history and a bit of humility, I'd add. It's not easy to reflect on our failures – the failures of Dot Com era ed-tech in this case – and move forward; but that's how we make progress.

It's important too to recognize the successes of the Dot Com era and to remember that, despite the failures of initiatives like AllLearn and Fathom, there were many online education programs founded in roughly the same period that didn't fold and that went on to be sustainable. Many of these continue to operate today.

I'd argue however that (sadly) that one of the most significant successes of the Dot Com ere – financial successes, that is – is one that has left an indelible mark on ed-tech. And that's the success of the learning management system. The technology, the industry.

While learning management system software predates the Internet, it was the Internet that became its big selling point. From *The Washington Post* in 1999: "Blackboard Chalks Up a Breakthrough; Its Educational Software Lets Colleges Put Classes on the Internet." (Several years, I'd like to point out, prior to the date in my opening anecdote when MIT supposedly offered the first course online.)

The LMS – or the VLE, I should say while here in the UK – has profoundly shaped how schools interact with the Internet. The LMS is a piece of administrative software. There's that word "management" in there that sort of gives it away for us in the US at least: that this software that purports to address questions about teaching and learning but that really works to "manage" and administer, in turn often circumscribing pedagogical possibilities. You can see its Dot Com roots too in the LMS functionality and in its interface. I mean, some LMSes still look like software from the year 2000! The LMS acts as an Internet portal to the student information system, and much like the old portals of the Dot Com era – much like AOL for example – it cautions you when you try to venture outside of it. You can access the LMS through your web browser but it is not really *of* the web.

The learning management system is a silo, a technological silo, by design. This isn't because the technology isn't available to do otherwise. Rather, it's a reflection of the institution of education. The LMS silo works because we tend to view each classroom as a closed entity, because we view each subject or discipline as atomistic and distinct. Closed. Centralized. Control in the hands of administrators, teachers, and IT but rarely in the hands of learners.

If you look at the much-hyped online courses of today – those offered on the Coursera or the edX platforms, for example – you can see the influence of the LMS. Each course you enroll in is separate, siloed. At the end of the term, your access to your course disappears. There's a tab on the LMS so you can navigate to the syllabus and a tab for assignments and one for assessments, and there is, of course – thanks early Internet technology! – a discussion forum. A message board. It isn't an accident, and it certainly isn't an innovation, that our online classes look this way.

It doesn't have to look this way, of course. There are other stories we could tell about education technology's past; there are other paths forward. Again, there's this hidden history of ed-tech (and of computer tech as well), and it's worth considering why so much has been forgotten or overlooked or dismissed. Ted Nelson. Douglas Englebart. Or the person I always point to: Seymour Papert.

Computers, argued Papert, should unlock children's "powerful ideas." That's the subtitle to his 1980 book *Mindstorms*, a book that I insist people in ed-tech read (although admittedly Papert's work is geared towards younger children rather than adult learners). *Mindstorms* addresses, "how computers can be carriers of powerful ideas and of the seeds of cultural change, how they can help people form new relationships with knowledge that cut across the traditional lines separating humanities from sciences and knowledge of the self from both of these. It is about using computers to challenge current beliefs about who can understand what and at what age. It is about using computers to question standard assumptions in developmental psychology and in the psychology of aptitudes and attitudes. It is about whether personal computers and the cultures in which they are used will continue to be the creatures of 'engineers' alone or whether we can construct intellectual environments in which people who today think of themselves as 'humanists' will feel part of, not alienated from, the process of constructing computational cultures."

Computers, Papert insisted, will help children gain "a sense of mastery over a piece of the most modern and powerful technology and establish an intimate contact with some of the deepest ideas from science, from mathematics, and from the art of intellectual model building."

But as we see with the LMS, ed-tech has come to mean something else. As Papert notes in his 1993 book *The Children's Machine*: "Progressive teachers knew very well how to use the computer for their own ends as an instrument of change; School knew very well how to nip this subversion in the bud."

"Computer-aided inspiration," as Papert envisioned, has been mostly trumped by "computer-aided instruction."

And we come full circle now to a technology I mentioned in passing at the beginning of my talk: PLATO, Programmed Logic for Automatic Teaching Operations, a computer system developed at the University of Illinois in the 1960s on its ILLIAC machine.

Early versions of the PLATO system had a student terminal attached to a mainframe. The software offered mostly "drill and kill" and tutorial lessons. But as the PLATO system developed, new and more sophisticated software was added. There were more problem-based lessons, for example. A new programming language called TUTOR enabled "anyone" to create their own PLATO lessons without having to be a programmer. The mainframe came to support multiple, networked computers. Students could communicate with one another, in addition to the instructor. And this was all pre-Internet, pre-Web.

This networked system made PLATO a site for a number of very important innovations in computing technology, not to mention in ed-tech. Forums, message boards, chat rooms, instant messaging, screen sharing, multiplayer games, and emoticons. PLATO was, as author Brian Dear argues in his forthcoming book *The Friendly Orange Glow* "the dawn of cyberculture."

But as with so much ed-tech history, PLATO's contribution to cyberculture is mostly forgotten. Yet we can still see remnants of PLATO in many of the features in ed-tech today, including of course, the learning management system. And if the learning management system has trapped us in a moment of Dot Com era tech – trapped in the old Internet portal – it may be that ed-tech's roots in PLATO have trapped us in an old "mainframe" mindset as well.

See, there are numerous legacies here. One of the features PLATO boasted: tracking every keystroke that a student made, data on every answer submitted, right or wrong. Sound familiar? PLATO offered more efficient computer-based testing. Sound familiar? It offered the broadcast of computer-based lessons to multiple locations, where students could work at their own pace. Sound familiar? Indeed, by the mid-Seventies, PLATO was serving students in over 150 locations – not just across the University of Illinois campus, but also in elementary schools, high schools, and on military bases.

Sensing a huge business opportunity – the notion of tapping into the giant "education market" is not new – the Control Data Corporation, the company that built the University of Illinois mainframe, announced that it was going to go to market with PLATO, spinning it out from a university project to a corporate one.

CDC charged $50 an hour for access to its mainframe, for starters. Each student unit cost about $1900; the mainframe itself $2.5 million, according to some estimates. CDC charged $300,000 to develop each piece of courseware. (So okay, I guess it *is* getting a little cheaper to develop courseware.)

Needless to say, PLATO as a commercialized computer-aided instruction product was largely a failure. The main success that CDC had with it: selling an online testing system to the National Association of Securities Dealers, a regulatory group that licenses stockbrokers.

Yet like the learning management system, the idea of computer-assisted instruction has retained an incredibly powerful hold over ed-tech. Indeed, as the history of PLATO shows us, the two are interconnected. Computer-based instruction. Computer-based management.

As we move forward, "building the digital institution," I think we must retrace and unwind some of these connections.

Why are we building learning management systems? Why are we building computer-assisted instructional tech? Current computing technologies demand neither. Open practices don't either. Rather, it's a certain institutional culture and a certain set of business interests that do.

What alternatives can we build? What can we imagine? Can we envision a future of learner agency, of human capacity, of equity, of civic responsibility, of openness for example?

I called this talk "Un-Fathom-able," thumbing my nose I confess at the failures of Fathom and what I think we may soon see as the failure of Coursera. I called this talk "Un-Fathom-able" too because I fear that there's much in ed-tech that we've failed to explore – partly, I would argue, that's because we have failed to learn and to reflect on the history of ed-tech. It's easy to blame technologists, I suppose. But I think all this runs deeper than that. There's been a failure of imagination to do something bold and different, something that, to borrow Papert's phrasing, unlocks "powerful ideas" in learners rather than simply re-inscribing powerful institutional mandates.

We can't move forward until we reconcile where we've been before.

This keynote was delivered on June 18, 2014 at CETIS in Bolton, UK. The original transcript, along with the slides for this talk, can be found on Hack Education at http://hackeducation.com/2014/06/18/unfathomable-cetis2014/

WORKS CITED

Yoni Appelbaum, "Digitalia Columbiana." *Columbia Daily Spectator.* January 30, 2003. http://columbiaspectator.com/2003/01/30/digitalia-columbiana

Mike Caulfield, "Experience Without Humility Is Not Very Helpful At All." April 16, 2014. http://hapgood.us/2014/04/16/experience-without-humility-is-just-experience/

Brian Dear, *The Friendly Orange Glow: The Story of the PLATO System and the Dawn of Cyberculture.* http://friendlyorangeglow.com/

D. D. Guttenplan, "Out in Front, and Optimistic, About Online Education." *The New York Times.* April 13, 2014. http://www.nytimes.com/2014/04/14/education/out-in-front-and-optimistic-about-online-education.html

Katie Hafner, "Lessons Learned at Dot-Com U." *The New York Times.* May 2, 2002. http://www.nytimes.com/2002/05/02/technology/lessons-learned-at-dot-com-u.html

Salman Khan and Michael Noer, "The History of Education." http://youtu.be/LqTwDDTjb6g

Tamar Lewin, "Coursera, an Online Education Company, Raises Another $43 Million." *The New York Times.* July 10, 2013. http://bits.blogs.nytimes.com/2013/07/10/coursera-an-online-education-company-raises-another-43-million/

Seymour Papert, *The Children's Machine: Rethinking School in the Age of the Computer.* Basic Books, 1993.

Seymour Papert, *Mindstorms: Children, Computers, and Powerful Ideas.* Basic Books. 1980.

3 TEACHING MACHINES: A BRIEF HISTORY OF "TEACHING AT SCALE"

Having spent the last week outside of the United States, in Europe talking about education technology, I have been reminded how much context matters. It matters when we talk about education technology's future, its present, and its history. Despite all the talk about the global economy, global communications, global democratization of education, context matters. The business and the politics and the stories of ed-tech are not universal.

I think that's something for you to keep in mind as you work your way through this course. It's something to think about when we start to imagine and to build "education at scale." What happens to context? What happens to local, regional education – its history, its content (the curriculum if you will), its cultural relevance and significance, and finally its politics, its practices?

How does technology shape this? How might technology erase or ignore context?

What ideologies does education technology carry with it? Do these extend, reinforce, or subvert existing ideologies embedded in education?

Because of the forward-facing ideology of technology – that is, its association with progress, transformation, "the future" – I think we do tend to forget its history. We tend to ignore its ideology. I think that dovetails quite powerfully too with parts of American ideology and identity: an emphasis on and excitement for "the new"; a belief that this country marked a formal break from other countries, from other histories. A belief in science and business and "progress."

Yesterday was one of those regularly scheduled moments when the technology industry puts all that ideology on display: an Apple keynote,

24

where new products are introduced that have everyone cooing about innovation, that have everyone prepared to declare last year's hardware and software obsolete, and often that have education technology writers predicting that new Apple products are going to revolutionize the way we teach and learn.

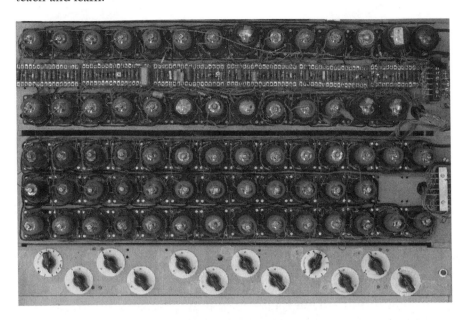

This image is not from the guts of the Apple Watch, of course, or the new iPhone. It is a close-up of the (rebuild of the) Colossus, the world's first electronic, programmable computer. The Colossus prototype was built at Bletchley Park, site of the British government's Code and Cypher School during World War II. It was used to help successfully decrypt German military communications.

Like I said, ideology is embedded in technology. Computers' origins are wrapped up in war and cryptography and surveillance. How does that carry forward into education technology?

When we talk about "education technology" we do tend to focus on the things that teachers and students can do with computers. But education technology certain pre-dates the Colossus (1943). And perhaps we could reach as far back to Plato's *Phaedrus* to see the sorts of debates about what the introduction of new technologies – in this classic example, Socrates' skepticism about the technology of writing – would do to education and more broadly, to culture.

I'm in the middle of writing a book called *Teaching Machines*, a cultural history of the science and politics of ed-tech. An anthropology of ed-tech even, a book that looks at knowledge and power and practices, learning and politics and pedagogy. My book explores the push for efficiency and automation in education: intelligent tutoring systems, artificially intelligent textbooks, robo-graders, and robo-readers.

This involves, of course, a nod to "the father of computer science" Alan Turing, who worked at Bletchley Park, and his profoundly significant question "Can a machine think?"

I want to ask in turn, "Can a machine teach?"

Then too: Why would we want a machine to teach? What happens, as this course is asking you to consider, when we use machines to teach and learn "at scale"?

And to Turing's question, what will happen to humans when (if) machines do "think"? What will happen to humans when (if) machines "teach"? What will happen to labor and what happens to learning?

And, what exactly do we mean by those verbs "think" and "teach"? When we see signs of thinking or teaching in machines, what does that really signal? Is it that our machines are becoming more "intelligent," more human? Or is it that humans are becoming more mechanical?

There's a tension there between freedom and standardization and mechanization that both technology and education grapple with.

Rather than speculate about the future, I want to talk a bit about the past.

I want to suggest that the history of education in the US (and again, this is why context really matters) is woven incredibly tightly with the development of education technologies, and specifically the development of teaching machines. Since the mid-nineteenth century, there have been a succession of technologies that were supposed to improve, if not entirely transform, the way in which teaching happened: the chalkboard, the textbook, radio, film, television, computers, the Internet, the Apple Watch, and so on.

There are a number of factors at play here that make education so susceptible to the technological influence. US Geography, for example: how do you educate across great distances? National identity: what role should schools play in enculturation, in developing a sense of American-ness? Should curriculum be standardized across the country? If so, how will that curriculum be spread? Individualism: how do we balance the desire to standardize education with our very American belief in individualism? How do we balance "mass education" with "meritocracy"? How do we rank and rate students? Industrialization: what is the relationship between schools and business? Should businesses help dictate what students should learn? Should schools be run like businesses? Can we make school more efficient?

These questions – how we've asked and answered them – shape the ways in which education technology has been developed and wielded.

Despite what you often hear that technologies will change teaching and learning, more likely technologies re-inscribe the traditional functions and practices of education.

For those interested in the history of education technology, I recommend Larry Cuban's book *Teachers and Machines*. He's better known for his book *Oversold and Underused*, which looks at computers and schools, but *Teachers and Machines* is interesting because you see the tension around technology in general. It's not simply teachers' reluctance to adopt computers, that is. His book looks at attempts to bring film (in the 1910s), radio (in the 1920s), and television (in the 1960s) into the classroom. These are all broadcast technologies, obviously. They're designed to "deliver educational content," a phrase I really hate. And they were all met with a certain amount of resistance.

Despite an emphasis on "content delivery systems," that's not to say that there weren't some really fascinating projects and predictions in the twentieth century. Take, for example, the Midwest Program on Airborne Television Instruction which operated two DC-6 aircraft out of Purdue University Airport using a technology called "Stratovision" to broadcast educational television to schools, particularly to those who couldn't otherwise pick up a TV signal.

I think there are some key lessons to be learned from these broadcast technologies. I think they're lessons that the MOOC providers, whose marketing sounds an awfully lot like some of these twentieth century "innovators," could do well to learn from. If nothing else, how much are we still conceptualizing technologies that "deliver content" and "expand access"? How does "broadcast" shape what we mean when we talk about "scaling" our efforts? How does "broadcast" fit neatly into very old educational practices centered on the teacher and centered on the content?

You could argue that film and radio and airborne television are "teaching machines," but typically the definition of "teaching machines" involves more than just "content delivery." It involves having an instructional and an assessment component as well. But again, these devices have a very long history that certainly predates computers.

The earliest known patent in the United States was issued in 1809 to H. Chard for a "Mode of Teaching to Read." The following year S. Randall filed a patent entitled "Mode of Teaching to Write." Halcyon Skinner (no relation to Harvard psychology professor B. F. Skinner) was awarded a patent in 1866 for an "Apparatus for Teaching Spelling." The machine contained a crank, which a student would turn until he'd arranged the letters to spell the word in the picture. The machine did not, however, give the student any feedback if it was right or wrong.

Between Halcyon Skinner's 1866 teaching machine and the 1930s, there were an estimated 600 to 700 patents filed on the subject of teaching and schooling. The vast majority of these were filed by inventors outside of the field of education. Halcyon Skinner, for example, also filed for a patent for a "motor truck for cars," "tufted fabric," a "needle loom," a "tubular boiler," and many other inventions.

There's some debate about whether or not these early devices "count" as teaching machines, as they don't actually do all the things that education psychologists later decided were key: continuous testing of what students are supposed to be learning; immediate feedback on whether a student has an answer correct; the ability for students to "move at their own pace"; automation.

American psychologist Sidney Pressey is generally credited with being the first person whose machine met all these requirements. He displayed a "machine for intelligence testing" at the 1924 meeting of the American Psychological Association. Pressey received a patent for the device in 1928.

His machine contained a large drum that rotated paper, exposing a multiple-choice question. There were four keys, and the student would press the number that corresponded to the right answer. Pressey's machine had two modes of operation: one labeled "test" and the other labeled "teach." In test mode, the machine would simply record the responses and calculate how many were correct. In teaching mode, the machine wouldn't proceed to the next question until the student got the answer right. The machine did still track how many keys were pressed until the student got it correct. You could also add an attachment to the machine that was essentially a candy dispenser. It allowed the experimenter to set what Pressey called a "reward dial," determining the number of correct responses required to receive a candy reward. Once the response criterion had been reached, the device automatically delivered a piece of candy to a container in front of the subject.

For a prototype that was converted from a sewing machine, we can see in Pressey's machine so much about 20th century education theory and practice – and so much of that that's still with us today. There's the connection to intelligence testing and the First World War and a desire to create a machine to make that process more standardized and efficient. There's the nod to the work of education psychologist Edward Thorndike: his laws of recency and frequency that dictated how students were supposed to move through material. There is the four answer multiple-choice question. How much of this is now "hard coded" into our education practices? How much of this is now "hard coded" into our education technology?

Sidney Pressey tried very hard to commercialize his teaching machines, but without much success. It wasn't until a few decades later that the idea really took off. And as such, "teaching machines" are probably most closely associated with the work of B. F. Skinner. (He did not receive the patent for his device until 1961.)

Skinner came up with the idea for his teaching machine in 1953. Visiting his daughter's fourth grade classroom, he was struck by its inefficiencies. Not only were all the students expected to move through their lessons at the same pace, but when it came to assignments and quizzes, they did not receive feedback until the teacher had graded the materials – sometimes a delay of days. Skinner believed that both of these flaws in school could be addressed through a machine, and built a prototype that he demonstrated at a conference the following year.

All these elements were part of Skinner's teaching machines: the elimination of inefficiencies of the teacher, the delivery of immediate feedback, the ability for students to move through standardized content at their own pace.

Today's ed-tech proponents call this "personalization."

Teaching – with or without machines – was viewed by Skinner as reliant on a "contingency of reinforcement." The problems with human teachers' reinforcement, he argued, were severalfold. First, the reinforcement did not occur immediately; that is, as Skinner observed in his daughter's classroom, there was a delay between students completing assignments and quizzes and their work being corrected and returned. Second, much of the focus on behavior in the classroom has to do with punishing students for "bad behavior" rather than rewarding them for good.

As Skinner wrote in his book *Beyond Freedom and Dignity*, "We need to make vast changes in human behavior. . . . What we need is a technology of behavior." Teaching machines are one such technology.

Skinner's teaching machine differed from Pressey's in that it did not have students push on buttons to respond to multiple-choice questions. Students had to manually enter their own answers. Skinner felt it was important that students could formulate their own responses. And he worried too that selecting the wrong answer on a multiple-choice question was the wrong sort of behavioral reinforcement.

As with Pressey's teaching machines, we can see in Skinner's some of these elements that still exist in our technologies today. Behaviorism in general: excitement about gamification and "nudges" and notifications from our apps all designed to get us to "do the right thing" (whatever that means). And we see too a real excitement about the potential for transforming classrooms with gadgetry.

"There is no reason," Skinner insisted, "why the schoolroom should be any less mechanized than, for example, the kitchen." Indeed in the 1960s, there was a huge boom in teaching machines. There were door-to-door teaching machine salesmen, I kid you not, including those who sold the Min-Max made by Grolier, the encyclopedia company.

But alongside the excitement were the fears about robots teaching the children. And the machines were expensive, as was the development of the "programmed instruction" modules.

So excitement faded, just as new devices started to be developed – ones that were computer-based. Ones that promises "intelligence."

Intelligence, along with all the promises that teaching machines have made for a century now: efficiency, automation, moving at your own pace, immediate feedback, personalization.

Thomas Edison predicted in 1913 that textbooks would soon be obsolete. In 1962, *Popular Science* predicted that by 1965, over half of students would be taught by machines. I could easily find similar predictions made today about MOOCs or adaptive technology or Apple Watches. These themes persist, and it's worth asking why.

I think you can explain a lot of it when you look at history and think about ideology – what we bring into our technologies, what we ask them to do, and how and why.

This talk was given to the Harvard Graduate School of Education class "The Future of Learning at Scale" on September 10, 2014. The original transcript can be found on Hack Education at http://hackeducation.com/2014/09/10/teaching-machines-teaching-at-scale/

WORKS CITED

Larry Cuban, *Oversold and Underused: Computers in the Classroom.* Harvard University Press, 2003.

Larry Cuban, *Teachers and Machines: The Classroom Use of Technology Since 1920.* Teachers College Press, 1986.

B. F. Skinner, *Beyond Freedom and Dignity.* Hackett Publishing Company, 1971.

B. F. Skinner, *The Technology of Teaching.* Copley Publishing Group. 1968.

"Teaching Machines: Do They Or Don't They?" *Popular Science.* 1962. Vol. 181, No. 6.

Alan Turing, "Computing machinery and intelligence." *Mind.* 1950. Vol. 59, 433-460.

II. THE IDEOLOGY OF ED-TECH

4 AGAINST "INNOVATION"

When I first was asked a couple of months ago to let the conference organizers know the title for my keynote today, I quickly glanced at the theme of the event and crafted some lengthy, semi-provocative phrase that would, I hoped, allow me to make the argument here that I make fairly often:

ORIGINAL KEYNOTE TITLE: SILICON VALLEY'S (ED-TECH) INNOVATION CULTURE VERSUS A CULTURE OF INNOVATIVE LEARNING

There's a significant divide – a political and financial and cultural and surely a pedagogical divide – between the technology industry (Silicon Valley in particular) and the education sector when it comes to thinking about the future of teaching and learning and also when it comes to thinking about the meaning of "innovation." As we move forward with our adoption of educational technologies, we must be more thoughtful, dare I say more vigilant about the implications of that divide.

The original title I offered focused on the word "culture" because, despite being a PhD dropout, I remain a scholar of culture and not a businessperson or a technologist (despite spending far too much timing writing and thinking about business and technology). I also wanted to skew slightly what's often the typical comparison made between technology companies and educational institutions: that the former are agile, readily pushing for and adapting to change, while the latter are ancient bureaucracies that are slow, if not utterly resistant to change.

This comparison leads people to say things like "culture eats strategy for breakfast," one of those pithy business guru sayings that you hear invoked to talk about change and leadership. In the case of education, "culture eats

32

strategy for breakfast" cautions business and technology leaders, and dare I say school administrators, that the slow-shifting nature of higher education will derail any plans for "innovation" unless that underlying culture can be addressed first. Change the culture of education. Then you can innovate. Or something like that.

So I thought initially that I'd like to talk to you today about the "culture" of innovators in tech and the "culture" of innovators in education (well, to be clear, those I'd label as innovators in education). Because even if both those groups are pushing for change, their values – their cultures – are incredibly different.

REVISED KEYNOTE TITLE: WHAT IS "SILICON VALLEY CULTURE" AND WHY THE HELL WOULD WE WANT IT ANYWHERE NEAR EDUCATION?

One culture values openness and collaboration and inquiry and exploration and experimentation. The other has adopted a couple of those terms and sprinkled them throughout its marketing copy, while promising scale and efficiency and cost-savings benefits. One culture values community, and the other reflects a very powerful strain of American individualism, not to mention California exceptionalism. One that touts personal responsibility, self-management, and autonomy.

One gives us something like YOUMedia, a learning space within the Chicago Public Library, where among other things, teens can learn programming and multimedia. And the other that gives us something like this:

Google Glass – a truly ostentatious eyepiece, a heads-up display that allows you to search and dictate and record and mostly look like an idiot, and of course allows Google to glean the metadata from your activity along the way – has become a symbol of what is, I think, a growing discomfort surrounding technology, innovation, and ideology. It's a "tech culture war" as the headline writers at Salon frequently call it.

"Glass Explorers" – that's Google's name for those in the pilot program. "Glassholes" is what others call the wearers. People wearing Google Glass in San Francisco – or more accurately, people wearing Google Glass into punk rock bars in the Lower Haight – have had the $1500 devices knocked off their faces. "Attacked!" the Explorers gasp, for videotaping people who don't want to be videotaped. Glassholes.

The private commuter buses for the employees of Google and Apple and other tech companies have become another lightning rod in this "tech culture war," symbols of privatization and inequality, with protests and blockades occurring regularly along their routes. As San Francisco-based writer Rebecca Solnit describes it:

"The Google Bus means so many things. It means that the minions of the non-petroleum company most bent on world domination can live in San Francisco but work in Silicon Valley without going through a hair-raising commute by car – I overheard someone note recently that the buses shortened her daily commute to 3.5 hours from 4.5. It means that unlike gigantic employers in other times and places, the corporations of Silicon Valley aren't much interested in improving public transport, and in fact the many corporations providing private transport are undermining the financial basis for the commuter train. It means that San Francisco, capital of the west from the Gold Rush to some point in the 20th century when Los Angeles overshadowed it, is now a bedroom community for the tech capital of the world at the other end of the peninsula."

As the investment dollars have flooded the Silicon Valley computer industry in recent years, the cost of living in what was already one of the world's most expensive cities has become out of reach for almost all its residents. The median rent for an apartment in San Francisco is now $3000 per month. The rent for a 2-bedroom apartment has gone up 33% in just the last two years. "Not a Single Home Is for Sale in San Francisco That an Average Teacher Can Afford," read a *Bloomberg Businessweek* headline earlier this year.

While paying lip service to "meritocracy," the myth that anyone who works hard enough can make it, the technology industry remains quite hostile to women. Just 13% of venture-capital funded startups are founded by women (that compares to about 30% of small businesses which are woman-owned). The industry also lacks racial diversity. 83% of VC funded startups are all white. Between 2009 and 2011, per capita income rose by 4% for white Silicon Valley residents and fell by 18% for Black residents.

As the (largely white, male) engineers and entrepreneurs pour in to

Silicon Valley looking to make their fortune – a recent survey found that 56% of computer engineers believe they'll become millionaires some day – what will happen to the culture of San Francisco?

Again, from Rebecca Solnit: "

All this is changing the character of what was once a great city of refuge for dissidents, queers, pacifists and experimentalists. Like so many cities that flourished in the post-industrial era, it has become increasingly unaffordable over the past quarter-century, but still has a host of writers, artists, activists, environmentalists, eccentrics and others who don't work sixty-hour weeks for corporations – though we may be a relic population. Boomtowns also drive out people who perform essential services for relatively modest salaries, the teachers, firefighters, mechanics and carpenters, along with people who might have time for civic engagement. I look in wonder at the store clerks and dishwashers, wondering how they hang on or how long their commute is. Sometimes the tech workers on their buses seem like bees who belong to a great hive, but the hive isn't civil society or a city; it's a corporation."

As I read Solnit's diary about the changes the current tech boom is bringing to San Francisco, I can't help but think about the changes that the current ed-tech boom might also bring to education, to our schools and colleges and universities. To places that have also been, in certain ways, a "refuge for dissidents, queers, pacifists and experimentalists."

Global ed-tech investment hit a record high this year: $559 million across 103 funding deals in the first quarter of the year alone. How does that shape or reshape the education landscape?

In the struggle to build "a great hive," to borrow Solnit's phrase, that is a civil society and not just a corporate society, we must consider the role that education has played – or is supposed to play – therein. What will all this investment bring about? Innovation? Innovation to what end?

When we "innovate" education, particularly when we "innovate education" with technology, which direction are we moving it? Which direction and why?

Why, just yesterday, an interview was published with Udacity founder Sebastian Thrun, who's now moving away from the MOOC hype and the promises he and others once made that MOOCs would "democratize education." Now he says, and I quote, "If you're affluent, we can do a much better job with you, we can make magic happen." Screw you, I guess, if you're poor.

I've gestured towards things so far in this talk that might tell us a bit about the culture of Silicon Valley, about the ideology of Silicon Valley.

But what is the ideology of "innovation"? The idea pre-dates Silicon Valley to be sure.

REVISED (AGAIN) KEYNOTE TITLE: THE IDEOLOGY OF INNOVATION

An aside: I have this tendency when I'm delivering a talk in Canada to be terribly inappropriate, to say things I shouldn't. Sometimes it's a deliberate provocation. Sometimes, it's accidental. Just as the words spill out of my mouth, I realize that I've failed to filter myself adequately. So I apologize.

REVISED (AGAIN) KEYNOTE TITLE: AGAINST INNOVATION

See, as I started to gather my thoughts about this talk, as I thought about the problems with Silicon Valley culture and Silicon Valley ideology, I couldn't help but choke on this idea of "innovation."

So I'd like to move now to a critique of "innovation," urge caution in chasing "innovation," and poke holes, in particular, in the rhetoric surrounding "innovation." I'd like to challenge how this word gets wielded by the technology industry and by extension by education technologists.

And I do this, I admit in part, because I grow so weary of the word. "Innovation" the noun, "innovative" the adjective, "innovate" the verb – they're bandied about all over the place, in press releases and marketing copy, in politicians' speeches, in business school professors' promises, in economists' diagnoses, in administrative initiatives. Um, in the theme of this conference and the name of this organization behind it. (Awkward.)

What is "innovation"? What do we mean by the term? Who uses it? And how? Where does this concept come from? Where is it taking us?

How is "innovation" deeply ideological and not simply descriptive?

Of course, a dictionary definition suggests that "innovation" might mean nothing more than "something new." According to *Merriam Webster* at least, innovation is "a new idea, a new method, a new device." It is "the act or process of introducing a new idea, a new method, a new device."

And on one hand, that means it's probably just fine that almost everything gets the "innovation" label slapped on it. I should just get over my frustrations with the word's over-usage. Because every day, there's something new. Every day is new. And as long as it's new, it's innovation! Especially if it's tied to technology.

Indeed, right there, embedded in this particular definition, is a nod to technology: "a new device."

What kind of technology? Well, here are *Merriam Webster*'s examples of how the word might be used in a sentence: "the latest innovation in computer technology" or "Through technology and innovation, they found ways to get better results with less work." Or "the rapid pace of technological innovation."

These examples help illustrate that, in popular usage at least, the new ideas, methods, and devices that comprise "innovation" have to do with computers. They also, let's note, have to do with labor, and they have to do with speed and efficiency. These examples highlight show how tightly bound "innovation" has become with technology and offer a hint perhaps as to why technologists are sometimes quick to conflate the adoption of new tools with the adoption of new ideas and practices. Technology counts as "innovation," even when we use it to do the same old stuff.

The *Merriam Webster Dictionary* definition of innovation leaves out the notion of "change." Defined this way, innovation isn't necessarily about transformational ideas, different methods. It's simply "a new thing." Innovation framed this way means perpetually buying or building new things. Shiny new things, new devices that – so conveniently – become rapidly obsolete. Strangely that's "innovation."

Using Google's Ngram Viewer, a tool that draws on the 5+ million books digitized by the company, we can trace the frequency of usage of "innovation." The origins of the word date back to the 16th century, but since the 1960s, its popularity has grown substantially.

The adjective "innovative" was hardly used before the 1960s at all. The timing here of its increasing usage, not surprisingly, coincides with the blossoming of the computer industry.

The *Oxford English Dictionary*, which also of course does a good job – but by some definitions, I suppose, a less "innovative" job – at showing how words and usage shift over time, does offer a definition of "innovation" that involves the idea of change: "The action of innovating; the introduction of novelties; the alteration of what is established by the introduction of new elements or forms."

Elements or forms, not devices.

Interestingly, here we have a mention of novelties, a word that connotes something that's newly popular but only for a short amount of time. The novelty doesn't last; nor does the "innovation." There's a need for constant, perpetual renewal.

Obsolete, according to the OED, the transitive version of the verb "innovate" – that is, "to innovate" used with a direct object, meaning "to change (a thing) into something new; to alter; to renew."

More common now, again according to the OED, the intransitive version of the verb – that is (a reminder for those who've forgotten their grammar lessons) an action verb that doesn't have a direct object that's the recipient of the action: "to innovate" meaning "to bring in or introduce novelties; to make changes in something established; to introduce innovations." "To innovate" simply is. It doesn't require a thing to act upon.

This makes the verb "to innovate" interesting to compare with "to invent," which does typically have a direct object. Again, using Google Ngrams, we can see that "to invent" remains far more popular. However, according to this tool, in the mid 1960s, "innovations" surpassed "inventions" in frequency of usage.

Wayne State University professor John Patrick Leary, who's writing a very wonderful Raymond Williams-esque blog series on "Keywords for the Age of Austerity" has looked closely at the history of the word "innovation" and suggests that we're actually seeing a return of its transitive usage, "to innovate" with a direct object.

He points, of course, to the *Harvard Business Review* which asks "Who's Innovating Innovation?" Leary adds that, "The transitive construction 'innovating innovation' thus uses the word in a form that was last common in the 18th century. Then, the word referred to a process of transformation or renewal that often carried religious implications: the salvation promised through Christ, but importantly also ... offered through deceit by false prophets."

Innovation as salvation. Or innovation as deception by false prophets. I'll return to this point later.

Today "innovation" has come to refer to commercial interests and entrepreneurial efforts, but a religious tinge to the word remains. Leary points to the intransitive usage in, for example, descriptions of Apple founder Steve Jobs: his "constant desire to innovate and take chances." Leary writes that, "We are no longer innovating on or upon anything in particular, which can make 'innovate' sound like a kind of mantra, recalling the religious associations the word once had: 'If you don't innovate every day and have a great understanding of your customers,' said a Denver processed cheese executive, 'then you don't grow.' Innovation sounds more and more like an epiphany here."

Innovation as mantra. Innovation as epiphany.

Another obsolete meaning of the word "innovation," according to the OED, incidentally, "A political revolution; a rebellion or insurrection" although perhaps, like the religious origins of the word, a bit of that meaning remains as well. Certainly we see the words "revolution" and "innovation" used almost interchangeably these days when it comes to technology marketing and the promise of transformation and upheaval and disruption. Although again, thanks to Google Ngrams, we can see the trajectory of those processes as they are talked about in literature. "Revolution" declines in frequency as "innovation" increases.

Of course, the technology innovation insurrection isn't a political one as much as it is a business one (although surely there are political ramifications of that).

In fact, innovation has been specifically theorized as something that will blunt revolution, or at least that will prevent the collapse of capitalism and the working class revolution that was predicted by Karl Marx.

That's the argument of economist Joseph Schumpeter who argued most famously perhaps in his 1942 book *Capitalism, Socialism and Democracy* that entrepreneurial innovation was what would sustain the capitalist system – the development of new goods, new companies, new markets that perpetually destroyed the old. He called this constant process of innovation "creative destruction."

Google Ngram suggests that the popularity of the phrase "creative destruction" follows a similar pattern to the word "innovation," picking up usage following World War II and growing exponentially in subsequent decades. A Harvard professor, Schumpeter and his ideas have been incredibly influential. One of his students was Alan Greenspan, the former chairman of the US Federal Reserve, who was known to invoke the term "creative destruction" when he spoke on Capitol Hill.

In the technology sector, Schumpeter's influence might best be known via the work of another Harvard professor, Clayton Christensen, who in 1997 published *The Innovator's Dilemma*, popularizing the phrase "disruptive innovation."

"Disruptive innovation." "Creative destruction."

The precise mechanism of the disruption and innovation in Christensen's theory differs from Schumpeter's. Schumpeter saw the process of entrepreneurial upheaval as something that was part of capitalism writ large. Industries would replace industries. Industries would always and inevitably replace industries.

Schumpeter argued this process of innovation would eventually mean the end of capitalism, albeit by different processes than Marx had predicted. Schumpeter suggested that this constant economic upheaval would eventually cause such a burden that democratic countries would put in place regulations that would impede entrepreneurship. He argued that, in particular, "intellectuals" – namely university professors – would help lead to capitalism's demise because they would diagnose this turmoil and develop critiques of the upheaval, critiques that would appealing and relevant to those beyond the professorial class.

That the enemy of capitalism in this framework is the intellectual and not the worker explains a great deal about American politics over the past few decades. It probably explains a great deal about the ideology behind a lot of the "disrupting higher education" talk as well.

Christensen offers a different scenario; there is no "end of capitalism" here. Christensen defines disruptive innovation as "a process by which a product or service takes root initially in simple applications at the bottom of a market" – that is, with customers who are not currently being served – "and then relentlessly moves up market, eventually displacing established competitors."

According to Christensen's framework, there are other sorts of innovations that aren't "disruptive" in this manner. There are, for example, "sustaining innovations," products and services that strengthen the position (and the profits) of incumbent organizations.

But that's not how the tech industry views itself today. It does not see itself as the makers of "sustaining innovations." Despite its growing economic and political power, the tech industry continues to see itself as an upstart not an incumbent. As a disruptor. An innovator.

The notion of "disruptive innovation" has resonated deeply with tech industry. It is worth pointing out, perhaps, that disk drive manufacturers were one of the case studies in Christensen's 1997 book. But Christensen himself has clarified that few technologies are intrinsically "disruptive technologies." Disruptive innovations, in fact, can be the result of what are fairly crude technologies. The innovation, he argues, instead comes from the business model.

That's why it doesn't matter to proponents of the "disruptive innovation" framework that Khan Academy or MOOCs suck, for example. It doesn't matter that they're low quality technologies featuring low quality instruction and sometimes low quality content. What matters is that they're free (or very, very cheap). What matters is that they change the market. It's all about markets after all. Students are consumers, not learners in this framework. What matters is that these innovations initially serve non-consumers (that is, students not enrolled in formal institutions) then "over time to march upmarket." That's why they're disruptive innovations, according to Christensen, who just this weekend published an op-ed in *The Boston Globe* insisting, "MOOCs' disruption is only beginning."

Innovating markets. Not innovating teaching and learning.

What interests me in Christensen's and Schumpeter's frameworks, I confess, aren't the business school analyses or business professors' case studies or predictions. What interests me, as I said at the beginning of this talk, is culture. What interests me are the stories that the businesses tell about "disruptive innovation" because this has become a near sacred story to the tech sector. It's a story of the coming apocalypse – destruction and transformation and redemption, brought to you by technology.

Again, these cultural remnants of an older meaning of "innovation," a process of transformation or renewal that has religious implications. Perhaps the salvation. Perhaps deception by false prophets. The Battles of the End Times, and you must decide which side you're on.

"The end of the world as we know it" seems to be a motif in many of the stories that we hear about what "disruptive innovation" will bring us, particularly as we see Christensen's phrase applied to almost every industry where technology is poised to transform it. The end of the newspaper. The end of the publishing industry. The end of print. The end of RSS. The end of the Post Office. The end of Hollywood. The end of the record album. The end of the record label. The end of the factory. The end of the union. And of course, the end of the university.

The structure to many of these narratives about disruptive innovation is well-known and oft-told, echoed in tales of both a religious and secular sort: Doom. Suffering. Change. Then paradise.

People do love the "end of the world as we know it" stories, for reasons that have to do with both the horrors of the now and the promise of a better future. Many cultures – and Silicon Valley is, despite its embrace of science and technology, no different here – tell a story that predicts some sort of cataclysmic event that will bring about a radical cultural (economic, political) transformation and, perhaps eventually for some folks at least, some sort of salvation.

The Book of Revelations. The Mayan Calendar. The Shakers. The Ghost Dance. Nuclear holocaust. Skynet. The Singularity.

Incidentally, and according to Google Ngrams at least, "innovation" surpassed "salvation" in popularity some time in the early 1970s – although both seem to be ticking upwards in unison.

I don't think this is an indication that "science" now trumps "religion" in late twentieth and early twenty-first century publications. As I hope I've illustrated for you, the stories that we tell about "innovation" are still very much tinged with faith.

But as I've tried to argue here and elsewhere, "innovation," and disruptive innovation in particular, does have this millennialist bent to it, a belief in transformation through destruction (and, if the tech industry libertarians have their way, through deregulation). What exactly does society look like on the other side of this change? What does education look like disrupted?

Again, as I've suggested in this talk, the answer to those questions will shape our culture. Our communities. And as such, the answers are political.

Our response to both changing technology and to changing education must involve politics – certainly this is the stage on which businesses already engage, with a fierce and awful lobbying gusto. But I worry that we put our faith in "innovation" as a goal in and of itself, we forget this. We confuse "innovation" with "progress" and we confuse "technological progress" with "progress" and we confuse all of that with progressive politics. We forget that "innovation" does not give us justice. "Innovation" does not give us equality. "Innovation" does not empower us.

We achieve these things when we build a robust civic society, when we support an engaged citizenry. We achieve these things through organization and collective action. We achieve these things through and with democracy. And we achieve – or we certainly strive to achieve – these things through public education.

41

This keynote was delivered at the Canadian Network for Innovation in Education conference, in Kamloops, BC on May 14, 2014. The original transcript, along with the slides which give you a better sense of the Google Ngrams discussed here, is available on Hack Education at http://hackeducation.com/2014/05/14/innovation-cnie-2014/

WORKS CITED

Clayton Christensen, *The Innovator's Dilemma.* Harper Business. 1997.

Clayton Christensen, "MOOCs' Disruption Is Only Beginning." *The Boston Globe.* May 9, 2014.

Carmel Deamicis, "A Q&A with 'Godfather of MOOCs' Sebastian Thrun after he disavowed his godchild," *Pando.* May 12, 2014 http://pando.com/2014/05/12/a-qa-with-godfather-of-moocs-sebastian-thrun-after-he-disavowed-his-godchild/

John Patrick Leary, "Innovation." *Keywords for the Age of Austerity.* February 27, 2014. http://jpleary.tumblr.com/post/78022307136/keywords-for-the-age-of-austerity-innovation

Joseph Schumpeter, *Capitalism, Socialism, and Democracy.* Harper Perennial Modern Classics. 1942.

Rebecca Solnit, "Diary." *London Review of Books.* February 2013. Vol. 35, No. 3. http://www.lrb.co.uk/v35/n03/rebecca-solnit/diary

Karen Weise, "Not a Single Home Is for Sale in San Francisco That an Average Teacher Can Afford," *Bloomberg Businessweek.* February 27, 2014. http://www.businessweek.com/articles/2014-02-27/theres-not-a-single-home-for-sale-in-san-francisco-that-an-average-teacher-can-afford

5 ENGAGING FLEXIBLE LEARNING

Thank you very much for inviting me here to speak to you. I spend a lot of time on the road; I attend and speak at a lot of conferences. It's always a pleasure to be at a conference that features educators and not just entrepreneurs, teachers and not just technologists.

It's always a pleasure to be at a conference that recognizes there is a long history to distance education, that Stanford University professors didn't "invent" online teaching or MOOCs just a couple of years ago.

Of course, it's always a pleasure to be in Canada, particularly BC. As my mum is from England and my dad is from the US, I always felt more Canadian than either British or American. Alas, my dad is from Wyoming, so I reckon that probably makes me more Albertan than British Columbian. But I do now live in Los Angeles, the best of all worlds: sunshine and a good hockey team.

I find it fascinating to visit other places and observe other countries or other provinces' education practices and politics. Too often, I think, we assume school has to be a certain way because that's the way *we* experienced it – historically as well as nationally. Yet everyone everywhere is confronted now with questions about education: about what education means, what education should look like now and in the future, and how we will pay for it.

It's somewhat consoling, I suppose, that the US isn't facing these challenges alone; yet it's wildly frustrating that we seem to have exported some of our shady policies and products and practices elsewhere in an attempt to shape that very future.

I've been asked to deliver the closing keynote here and respond to what I've seen and heard over the last few days. As someone who thrives on debates about education technology, I really, really like having the final word. So again, thank you. But when I give the last word – heck any word –

it tends to be a little dark, a little grave, a little provocative, a little pessimistic. So I apologize in advance.

I am a pessimist about education and technology (I hope, I try) in the tradition of Neil Postman and Leo Marx and David Noble. I am a "a pessimist," to quote Antonio Gramsci, "because of intelligence, but an optimist because of will." I don't think education technology is *de facto* awful but I do think late capitalism, neoliberalism, and technological imperialism generally are.

I want to frame my remarks – a mix of optimism and pessimism and a full blast of politics – around the theme of the conference: Engaging Flexible Learning.

That's two adjectives and a gerund. Or a present participle, an adjective, and a gerund. Those three words have multiple meanings and as such the phrase "engaging flexible learning" has several interpretations. (As you can see, my formal academic background is in language and literature. I have a degree in Folklore not one from a business or engineering or education school. I study culture and stories.) I want to reflect on this phrase and these terms and ask a bunch of questions – questions that don't have easy answers but that you (we, all of us) need to stew on as we leave this event and as we move forward into a world of shifting educational technologies and shifting educational practices and – this is key – shifting educational politics and power.

LEARNING

Let's start with "learning."

It's a relief – truly – to be at a conference where "learning" appears not just in its name and in session titles, but that has been fundamental to many of the conversations that were held here over the last few days. We do spend an inordinate amount of time in education and in education technology talking about things other than learning. We talk about the tech, for example, using that as a proxy for learning. We talk about administration and management. We talk about efficiency. We talk about enrollments. We talk about data points and learning objects and content repositories. We talk about instruction, using that as a proxy for learning. We talk about assessment, using that as a proxy for learning.

It was, of course, President George W. Bush who famously observed, "Rarely is the question asked: Is our children learning?"

Shortly afterwards, he proposed the No Child Left Behind Act, federal legislation which when enacted in 2001 helped usher in the US's current era of high stakes standardized testing, an era in which we still find ourselves, an era in which what happens in school in the US has been greatly circumscribed as so much time and money and energy is spent on prepping for and administering the mandated language arts and math assessments.

With a grammatically twisted phrase, Bush asked, "Is our children learning"; no surprise, what we got in response was a system that gave us a twisted answer.

We continue to struggle with all this testing madness in the US – and we're doing our best (along with that education behemoth Pearson. Thanks Britain!) to export this madness worldwide. Education and empire. Some things never change, do they.

Despite all this, you'll hear many folks, myself included, insist that we now find ourselves in an era of remarkable potential for education. It is a great time to be a learner thanks in no small part to new technologies: the Internet, the World Wide Web, ubiquitous mobile phones and other cheaper computing devices. These technologies offer us exciting opportunities for learning new things in new ways with new people, for extending capacity and access, for as David Porter argued in his keynote yesterday "openness."

And yet we see much of this exuberance for learning happening in informal settings, not in formal education institutions. Watching YouTube videos at home so we can learn to play an instrument or make sushi or fix a leaky faucet, for example. Creating videos, writing blogs, making graphics or music and sharing them online. Supporting peers who want to learn how you did those things. Having a wide range of free, openly licensed educational material available online, along (again) with peers and mentors to work with through it. Joining the Maker Movement. Building with hardware and software and electronics and cardboard. Playing Minecraft. Pursuing your own interests to your own end, building on your own experiences and discoveries. Exploring and experimenting. Learning.

It's hard not to look at all this without thinking of, without invoking the American educator, psychologist, and philosopher John Dewey. As he wrote in 1938 in *Experience and Education*, "There is no such thing as educational value in the abstract. The notion that some subjects and methods and that acquaintance with certain facts and truths possess educational value in and of themselves is the reason why traditional education reduced the material of education so largely to a diet of predigested materials."

Computer technologies, many have argued, provide us with an opportunity to rethink and revise "traditional education," to break free of old or outmoded practices – particularly if you frame the change in Dewey's terms at least – so as to make learning more meaningful.

And framed that way, I think "is our children learning?" is clearly the wrong question. With our (American) obsession with counting stuff, with measuring stuff, the wrong question means too the wrong "answer."

So what does "flexibility" have to do with that? What do we mean by the second word in the conference theme, "flexible"?

How do we make our schools more flexible? How do we balance the need to change with what's often an institutional reluctance to do so?

What does "flexible learning" entail? What does "flexibility" afford us? What does it afford schools, teachers, administrators, parents, sure. What does it afford students? What are the repercussions – for individuals, for communities?

Does flexibility mean the removal of silos in education that make collaboration across subjects and across grades and across school buildings so difficult? How do we best support that sort of flexibility? Who gets support? How? Why?

Does flexibility include challenging "seat time" – that is, ending the practice whereby school funding is allocated, a student's progress is measured, and degrees are awarded based on the number of hours and weeks spent in class?

Will computer technology be the lever we use to reframe how students move through material, focusing as some suggest, on "mastery" of skills and concepts and "competencies"? What lessons can we learn from "competency-based programs" of the past so that we don't make the same mistakes again? I think here of the GED, or high school equivalency test. What's the point of the GED: passing the test or learning? What does the GED really tell us? What does the GED mean?

Does flexibility mean that learners have control of their learning? Does it mean they have agency in determining their learning path? (And I don't mean here simply having the option to a choose between learning French or Chinese, although certainly the Internet does afford opportunities to learn Chinese whereas before there might have been no choice at all.)

Does flexibility mean that learners get to decide what "skills and concepts and 'competencies'" matter to them? Or are these still going to be imposed on learners? Again, flexible how? Flexible for whom?

Is flexibility code for "school choice," a politically-loaded phrase that in the US at least is associated with giving families opportunities to "choose" where their children attend school, as a result sometimes funneling taxpayer dollars away from public schools and into private, sometimes for-profit, sometimes online, sometimes religious schools.

Is flexibility code for ending or exempting schools from regulations? And which schools, which regulations might those be? Again, what do we know about the history of lifting regulations surrounding education and distance education? What can we do to make that process more just?

With "flexible learning," are we pursuing Dewey's vision of the future of education or are we pursuing Bush's vision? Not just the policies of George W Bush but of his little brother, digital learning advocate and presidential hopeful Jeb Bush.

ENGAGING

But that's why this last term in the conference theme – "engaging" – is so very important.

I'm going to take the liberty here of interpreting "engaging" a certain way. Not as an adjective modifying "learning." I don't mean "engaging" as in "interesting or riveting." I don't mean "oh hey, I paid attention" so someone somewhere gets to tick off this lesson as "engaging."

Engagement is deep and difficult. Indeed, I believe that learning requires engagement otherwise learning isn't likely to occur. Maybe memorization can happen, but not deep and transformative learning.

I'm not interpreting the term "engaging" here as in the Captain Jean Luc Picard sense of "Engage!" Onward with unquestioning obedience.

I don't mean "engagement" as in some sort of long-term legal commitment between technology companies and schools. "I swear to honor and obey these Terms of Service 'til our profit margins insist we doth part."

"Engage" doesn't mean "embrace" "Engaging" means "grappling with" and "debating." It means contestation and criticism. Not simply cheering. "Engaging" implies that there is discussion to be had about the shape our policies and practices take. This isn't about passive or unquestioning adoption of new technologies; it's about actively wrestling with difficult questions about what these technologies might mean, about who benefits and how.

Whether we like it or not, education is an incredibly political topic. Education is a political effort, partially of course because of the role that governments – local, provincial, federal – play in rules and regulation and funding mechanisms. And partially because one of the goals of education in a democracy is to produce citizens.

Education is political too because of the *polis*, the connections between education and community. Education is political because learning is at once personal (and, of course, "the personal is political") and social; it is both a private and a public act.

Education is political. And so "engage" we must.

Taking an approach to ed-tech that is tinged with criticism and asking others to be skeptical about ed-tech might sound like a ridiculous thing to suggest we do at an ed-tech conference. And it's probably frustratingly annoying advice to give those who've had to argue for decades now that computing technologies are something we want and need in schools.

Doubly frustrating: despite our making these arguments for decades, we still face resistance from those who think there is no place for computers in the classroom, those who think the Internet should be blocked at school, those who see computers as distractions or as toys and not, as Seymour Papert put it, "powerful machines."

But education technology criticism isn't anti-ed-tech. It is not anti-computer. It is not anti-technology. Calling for what he called "computer criticism," Papert argued that, "The name does not imply that such writing would condemn computers any more than literary criticism condemns literature or social criticism condemns society. The purpose of computer criticism is not to condemn but to understand, to explicate, to place in perspective. Of course, understanding does not exclude hard (perhaps even captious) judgment. The result of understanding may well be to debunk. But critical judgment may also open our eyes to previously unnoticed virtue."

The words and the work of Seymour Papert guide much of what I do and think and write about when it comes to ed-tech. If you follow me on Twitter or read my blog, you'll hear me shout "Read *Mindstorms*!" a lot.

But I feel as though we are in a different world now than when Papert wrote his famous book. *Mindstorms* was first published in 1980 for crying out loud. In it, Papert argued that the age of the personal computer would be utterly transformational to the way in which we learn, the way in which school is organized.

We haven't listened to Papert. Sadly, quite to the contrary, we've ignored him, even when computers have been adopted in schools.

But in the meantime, since *Mindstorms'* publication, things have changed. Technologies have advanced. We are closer to Papert's vision of a computing device in every child's hand.

But the politics of technology have changed as well, a reflection of the growing power of the tech industry. And let's be frank here, the tech industry has its sights set on education – as a market, as an ideology, as something to automate, something to "fix," something to "disrupt."

"Education is broken," we hear from Silicon Valley. "Education is a bubble," we hear from Silicon Valley. "Education is ripe for disruption," we hear from Silicon Valley. "Buy our product," we hear from Silicon Valley.

And what in turn is Silicon Valley buying?

Google, for example, spent almost $16 million lobbying the US federal government in 2013. It was outspent by only 11 other organizations, including several in the telecommunications sector, namely AT&T and Comcast. (Google was the fifth highest spender the previous year, in 2012.)

And we've seen the laws governing marketing and advertising and children change, often in ways that are beneficial to companies like Google. We've seen partnerships between these companies and the US government promoting digital textbooks, Internet connectivity, and educational software.

As David Porter noted yesterday, Facebook's mission is "to give people the power to share and make the world more open and connected." Do we really believe that Google and Facebook and similar companies want us connected to the Internet out of some sort of corporate altruism? Do we really think they want to be involved in education "for the sake of the children"? Both those companies have their hands in MOOCs, of course. Google employs both Sebastian Thrun, the founder of Udacity and Andrew Ng, the co-founder of Coursera, two of the major MOOC startups out of Stanford. Google has partnered with Udacity. Facebook has partnered with edX. Why?

The ideology of the technology sector and of Silicon Valley is something that educators need to pay more attention to, I'd argue. We need to ask more "Why?" All this talk of "disruptive innovation" – who does Silicon Valley think needs to be disrupted? How does Silicon Valley define innovation? How does it define "engaging flexible learning"?

Education technology startups have raised a record amount of venture capital funding in the first quarter of this year. In the first three months of 2014, companies raised over $559 million across 103 deals. Ted Mitchell, the CEO of NewSchool Venture Fund, one of the major investment firms funding charter schools and ed-tech startups, has been nominated by President Obama as the Under Secretary of Education.

How does this influx of investment and investors shape – or hope to shape – education?

As Neil Selwyn writes in his recent book *Distrusting Educational Technology*, "While undoubtedly of great potential benefit, it is clear that educational technology is a value-laden site of profound struggle that some people benefit more from than others – most notably in terms of power and profit."

We have to ask the difficult questions of technology, even those of us who consider ourselves advocates of technology.

We have to ask about student data, student privacy. We have to ask who owns student data, who controls it, who profits from collecting and analyzing it. (Spoiler alert: the answer here isn't "the student.")

We have to ask more questions about the collection and analysis of student data that is feeding algorithms that promise "personalization." What do technology companies actually mean by "personalization"? We have to consider if we are reducing students from people to profiles. And we must ask these questions, knowing full well that education institutions have never really done a good job recognizing students as people.

How might the marketing promise surrounding "personalization" steer us away from self-direction and into pre-determined, pre-ordained pathways? Can we have "personalization" if it's built on top of standardized of content?

If, as I said at the beginning of this talk, this is a great time to be a self-directed learner, how might technology be used to dull rather than empower learner agency?

What are the repercussions of competency-based and mastery-based learning? What are the repercussions of choice? What are the repercussions of distance? What are the repercussions of scaling? Who gains? Who gains from "choice"? How do we reconcile the individual's needs – how the individual benefits – from society's needs?

I ask this because the ideology of computer technologies is radically individualistic. There's a very powerful strain of American individualism that permeates technology: personal responsibility, self-management, autonomy. All that sounds great when you frame this – as I have repeatedly in this talk – in terms of self-directed learning. But how do we reconcile that individualism with the social and political and community development that schools are also supposed to support? How do we address these strains of individualism and libertarianism – anti-institutional, anti-governmental, and pro-"free market"? What do we do about the ways in which these ideologies are embedded deeply within many aspects digital technology in society?

In a recent talk at the DLD conference in Munich, Evgeny Morozov, author of *To Save Everything, Click Here*, argued that "We are losing the ability to talk about things at the level of the collective." Morozov links this to neoliberalism, to American individualism exported around the world, to technology – as ideology and infrastructure – to the idea that we throw all of our problems to the markets, to venture capitalists, to bankers.

If the personal computer has heightened this today, might "personalization" via ed-tech inscribe this more deeply for tomorrow?

Markets don't work at the level of citizens. Markets work at the level of consumers. Markets – big markets, the ones that raise over half a billion dollars in venture funding – don't work at the level of community. Markets value competition. Collusion sometimes sure, but not really collaboration.

And so here we are. Do we empty out our ability to come together as a community because we believe, as Morozov has argued, in "technology solutionism," that somehow apps can solve the very difficult problems that we've struggled with for centuries, the very difficult problems that we've created ourselves as "21st century problems." Poverty. Environmental destruction. Education. Rather than "engaging" with these challenges through debate, through democracy, we opt for an app. We choose the "easy button," not because it works, but because it's bright and shiny and implores us to "click here."

There are other stories, of course. Technology doesn't have to look like that. I want to give a shout out here to Edward Hewlett, the head of technology at the Traditional Learning Academy, who held a workshop yesterday on his "experiment" – that's what he called it – using Minecraft.

When people ask me what I'm excited about in ed-tech, Minecraft is one of my go-to answers. It's not a flashcard app. It's not a learning management system. It's not a digital textbook. It's not a learning analytics platform. Minecraft is an open-ended virtual playground.

It's a deceptively simple world – "blocky" I think you'd call it – with graphics that make some adults sneer and say, "Oh my kids would never play with that." But kids do. They love it.

Minecraft isn't a game. Not really. There are rules, sure. To survive, you have to collect resources and build shelter. You have to build before night falls because at night, there are monsters. But that's it, really. There aren't levels to beat. There isn't a "save the princess" narrative. The world you build and narrate is up to you.

The world that Edward Hewlett built with his school, a Christian online school, is particularly interesting. Hewlett initially envisioned building something that echoed some of his early experiences in virtual worlds – the good and the frustrating. He wanted to address something he felt was missing in a "distributed school": a playground. He wanted to give his students a place to play and explore and learn, to figure out the "mechanics" of Minecraft and from there, to build their own virtual world.

And it wasn't simple. It wasn't easy. Hewlett and his students have built beautiful buildings and beautiful cities. They've created transportation systems. They've developed a virtual economy.

But there were challenges. A student vandalized Things. Virtual items were destroyed. Hewlett's Minecraft character became the target of a virtual assassination attempt. And accusations flew. The online community was in peril.

Hewlett's response is noteworthy. It's certainly possible, through various add-ons and modifications, for the owner of a Minecraft server to wield complete and total technical power, to track every click and every brick that students placed, for example, to prevent students from interacting or modifying or destroying others' creations,

Hewlett didn't opt to do that. As he put it in the workshop yesterday, he chose the "moral solution" instead of the technical one. He worked on strengthening the community. He helped the students develop their own governance – human rules not programmatic ones. Human capacity for care and community-building, not technological solutionism.

Engagement. Political, community, and intellectual engagement.

If you've played Minecraft or if you have kids who play Minecraft, you probably know the hours and hours and hours and hours of work that go into building and exploring in that world – much more time, I'd wager, than what students probably spend on other school projects, essays, and so on. There is learning there. A great deal of learning. Take a look at the videos on YouTube, for example, and you'll see a wonderful example of networks of learning and sharing. But it's hard to assess via a standardized test. It's messy too, all that community building and the building building. A Creeper can come along and destroy everything.

But such is learning at its best. Frustrating. Messy. Open-ended. Fragile.

When George W. Bush quipped, "rarely is the question asked, 'Is our children learning?'" he demanded schools answer by measuring more stuff, by focusing on "the data." That obsession for measurement dovetails nicely with computing technologies. We are now creating data at an unprecedented scale, with unprecedented velocity and increasing complexity. The temptation is to believe that if we can just collect all the data from our students – all their clicks – run it through an algorithm, do a little pattern-matching, and we'll solve everything, we'll unlock the secrets of the human brain, we'll unlock the potential of each child.

But it's not that easy. Learning – human learning – isn't an algorithm. The problems we face surrounding education cannot be solved simply by technology. They require political debate and democratic engagement. They require morals not markets. They require flexibility. They require compassion. They require justice. They require great care.

Education is a human endeavor – profoundly human. We cannot, we should not automate these processes with teaching machines. Because we are tasked with teaching people after all.

This keynote was given on April 9, 2014 at the BC Digital Learning Conference in Vancouver, British Columbia. The original transcript can be found on Hack Education at http://hackeducation.com/2014/04/09/bc-digital-learning-conference-2014/

WORKS CITED

John Dewey, *Experience and Education*. Free Press. 1938.

Evgeny Morozov, "Against Solutionism." DLD. January 20, 2014. http://youtu.be/uhU0hRng-eE

Seymour Papert, "Computer Criticism vs. Technocentric Thinking." *Educational Researcher*. January/February 1987. Vol 16, No. 1.

Seymour Papert, *Mindstorms: Children, Computers, and Powerful Ideas*. Basic Books. 1980.

Neil Selwyn, *Distrusting Educational Technology: Critical Questions for Changing Times*. Routledge, 2013.

6 ROBOTS AND EDUCATION LABOR

There's this notion, one that's becoming more and more pervasive I think, that the "real reason" you go to school is to gain "skills" so you can "get a good job." The purpose of education at the K-12 and the college level: job training and career readiness.

As such, there's a growing backlash against the liberal arts and particularly against the humanities. The President sneers at art history majors. Florida governor Rick Scott suggests we charge those who study philosophy or anthropology more for tuition. California gubernatorial candidate Neel Kashkari wants to make tuition free for students majoring in science, technology, engineering or math, in exchange for a small – and unspecified – percentage of their future earnings.

My background, I confess, is in the humanities. I write about education technology for a living, but I have no formal academic training from a School of Engineering or a School of Business or a School of Education. What I do have is an interdisciplinary undergraduate degree and a master's degree in Folklore. I'm a PhD Candidate in Comparative Literature, a PhD Candidate for life as I am an academic dropout. I have a love of storytelling and many years' training in thinking about narratives, culture, and power. That makes me wildly unemployable in some people's eyes, I guess; perhaps it makes me, in their eyes, incredibly critical and as such wildly dangerous. (Or at least I like to imagine I'm dangerous.)

And no doubt, it's the literary scholar in me that compels me to invoke Karel Čapek to open a discussion about education, labor, and technology.

In 1920, Čapek – or by some accounts his brother Josef – coined the term "robot" for the play *Rossum's Universal Robots* or *R.U.R.* The word comes from the Czech "roboti" which meant "serf labor." "Drudgery," another translation offers. Or, via Wikipedia, "the amount of hours a serf owed his master in a given day."

The robots in Čapek's play aren't the metallic machines that the word conjures for us today. They're more biological, assembled out of a protoplasm-like substance.

In the play's first act, a young woman named Helena, daughter of an industry mogul, arrives at the island factory where the robots are built. She's come as part of the League of Humanity, there to argue that the robots have souls and that they should be freed. The robots, which work faster and cheaper than humans (actually, the robots aren't paid at all), have quickly taken over almost all aspects of work. They remember everything, but they do not like anything. "They make great university professors," observes Harry Domin, the general manager of the robot factory.

As the play progresses, robots come to dominate all aspects of the economy, and the human birth rate falls. The robots stage a rebellion – a global rebellion as, unlike humans, robots share a universal language and recognize the universality of their labor struggles. Hoping to stop the economic and political crisis, Helena burns the formula for building robots. The robots kill all the humans, save one man in the factory who still works with his hands.

But then the robots discover that without the formula Helena has destroyed, they cannot re-produce. The play ends with the dismayed robot rebels recognizing that "The machines are turning out nothing but bloody chunks of meat."

Čapek's play was translated into over thirty languages and performed all over the world. The success of the play came no doubt because in the 1920s it struck a nerve with regards to fears of automation, industrialization, war, and revolution. The play demands the audience consider what is happening to our humanity as a result of these.

Indeed that's the question that robots always raise: what is happening to our humanity? As we mechanize and now digitize the world around us, what happens to our labor, our love, our soul? Are we poised to find ourselves reduced to "bloody chunks of meat"?

Certainly there are those who argue that automation will make the world more efficient, that automation will save us – or at least save the corporations money. There are those that insist that automation is inevitable. "We are entering a new phase in world history – one in which fewer and fewer workers will be needed to produce the goods and services for the global population," write Erik Brynjolfsson and Andrew McAfee in their book *Race Against the Machine*. "Before the end of this century," says *Wired Magazine*'s Kevin Kelly, "70 percent of today's occupations will ... be replaced by automation." *The Economist* offers a more rapid timeline. "Nearly half of American jobs could be automated in a decade or two," it contends.

The technologies that Brynjolfsson and McAfee and Kelly and others point to might be new: self-driving cars and military drones and high-speed trading and mechanized libraries and automated operating rooms. But their arguments about the coming age of robots are not, as Čapek's play – almost one hundred years old now – reminds us. And as *Rossum's Universal Robots* highlights as well, the hopes and fears about the implications of labor-saving devices are in many ways inextricably connected to our hopes and fears about labor itself.

Which jobs will be automated? And why? You can't answer these questions by simply saying "Oh, it'll be the jobs that are the easiest to automate." Automating surgery, automating warfare isn't "easy." We pursue the automation of certain jobs because they are routine-heavy, sure. We automate certain small tasks at first, but then all of work changes around that. We pursue the automation of some tasks because they are jobs we simply do not want to do, or that we do not want humans to have do. We seek to automate some workplace environments because we want efficiency. In other settings, we seek a more programmable, controllable – perhaps a more docile – workforce.

As such, a robot work-force is often embodied and gendered in ways that reflect how we value work, whose work is valued.

This makes the automation of education particularly interesting – and, I think, particularly troubling.

You often hear politicians and venture capitalists and education technology entrepreneurs insist that they don't want to replace teachers; they just want to enhance their capabilities through new technologies. (Well, you do hear some folks explicitly say we're going to replace teachers with technology, don't get me wrong. But most don't state it so boldly or so publicly.)

Adaptive learning software. Automated grading tools. Proponents of these tools want to be able to assess and engineer the classroom so that it works more efficiently. While decrying schools as being based on a "factory model" of production, their efforts sometimes look like an attempt to just update the pacing of the assembly line, so that students can move through it "at their own pace."

Again, they might boast cutting-edge technology, but the politics and the business and the ideology that underlie these endeavors are not new. Indeed, the drive to create "teaching machines" occupied researchers and businessmen for much of the 20th century.

We can trace some of the early efforts to automate education back before Čapek coined the term "robot." To a patent in 1866 for a device to teach spelling. Or a patent in 1909 for a device to teach reading. Or a patent in 1911 awarded to Herbert Aikens that promised to teach "arithmetic, reading, spelling, foreign languages, history, geography, literature or any other subject in which questions can be asked in such a way as to demand a definite form of words ... letters ... or symbols."

We could trace these efforts to automate education back to a machine developed by Sidney Pressey. Pressey was psychologist at Ohio State University, and around 1915 he came up with an idea to be able to use a machine to score the intelligence tests that the military was using to determine eligibility for enlistment. Then World War I happened, causing a delay in Pressey's research.

Pressey first exhibited his teaching machine at the 1925 meeting of the American Psychological Association. It had four multiple-choice questions and answers in a window and four keys. If the student thought the second answer was correct, he pressed the second key; if he was right, the next question was turned up. If the second answer was not the right one, the initial question remained in the window, and the student persisted until he found the right one. A record of all the student's attempts was kept automatically.

Intelligence testing based on students' responses to multiple-choice questions. Multiple-choice questions with four answers. Automated grading and data collection. Sound familiar?

Harvard professor B. F. Skinner claimed he'd never seen Pressey's device when he developed his own teaching machine in the mid-1950s. Indeed, he dismissed Pressey's inventions, arguing they were *testing* and not *teaching* machines. Skinner didn't like the multiple choice questions. His teaching machine enabled students to enter their own responses by pulling a series of levers. A correct answer meant a light would go on.

A behaviorist, Skinner believed that teaching machines could provide an ideal mechanism for what he called "operant conditioning." Education as mechanized behavior modification. "There is no reason why the schoolroom should be any less mechanized than, for example, the kitchen," Skinner said.

He argued that immediate, positive reinforcement was key to shaping behavior. And he argued that, despite their important role in helping to shape student behavior, "as a mere reinforcing mechanism, the teacher is out of date."

I'll ask again: why do we seek to automate certain tasks, certain jobs? Whose work is "out-of-date"?

For us, Skinner's teaching machine might look terribly out-of-date, but I'd argue that this is the history that still shapes so much of what we see today built with fancier components, newer hardware and software. Self-paced learning, gamification, an emphasis on real time or near-real-time corrections.

No doubt, education and education technology both draw so heavily on Skinner because Skinner (and his fellow education psychologist Edward

Thorndike) have been so influential in how we view teaching and learning, in how we view testing, in how we construct schooling. This isn't something that just affects K-12 schools either.

When we talk about the types of jobs that will be automated, you could argue that education will be safe. Education is, after all, about relationships, right? You could maintain that education is based on an ethic of care, and humans remain superior to machines when it comes to caring for other humans.

But as the efforts of Skinner and Thorndike and others would suggest, that isn't the only way, or even the predominant way, to view the "work" that happens in education. Rather than seeing learning as a process of human inquiry or discovery or connection, the focus becomes instead on "content delivery." And "content delivery" can surely be automated.

Let me turn again to popular culture and to science fiction. The latter in particular helps us tease out these things: the possibilities, horrors, opportunities of technology and science. I turn to science fiction because novelists and playwrights and researchers and engineers and entrepreneurs construct stories using similar models and metaphors. "Robot" appeared first in science fiction, let's remember. I refer to science fiction because what our culture produces in the film studio or at the writer's desk is never entirely separable from what happens in the scientist's lab, what happens at the programmer's terminal. We are bound by culture. And there are some profoundly important – and I would add, terribly problematic – views on teaching and learning that permeate both science fiction and technological pursuits.

The view of education as a "content delivery system," for example, appears as readily in ed-tech companies' press releases as it does on the big screen. Take *The Matrix* where Keanu Reeves delivers one of his finest lines as a computer injects directly into his brainstem all the knowledge he needs: "Whoa, I know Kung Fu."

This desire – based much more on science fiction than on science – for an instantaneous learning pill is something that many in ed-tech pursue. MIT Media Lab founder Nicholas Negroponte, speaking at this year's main TED event, predicted that in the next 30 years, we'll literally be able to ingest information. We'll swallow a "learning pill" that will deliver knowledge to the brain, helping you learn English, for example, or digest all of Shakespeare's works. That's some seriously speculative bullshit.

But preposterous or not, this long-running plot line in science fiction dovetails neatly with renewed promises of efficiency through the automation of education. And it connects to a long-standing goal of artificial intelligence in education: the creation of AI-backed machines that claim to automate and "personalize" lesson delivery and assessment. And now, we need look no further than the recent MOOC craze, with its connections to the AI labs at Stanford – that's where Udacity co-founder Sebastian Thrun and Coursera co-founders Andrew Ng and Daphne Koller work – and at MIT -- that was where edX head Anant Agarwal worked.

Of course, the AI in MOOCs remains incredibly crude. These courses use mostly multiple-choice assessments, for example. They rarely seem to pay attention to signals from our data. If you've signed up for a MOOC, I'm sure you've received a number of emails announcing it's Week 5, or something, "so keep up the good work," when you've never logged in after you signed up. Or all those emails suggesting you sign up for more MOOCs. Maybe you'd like a class on sports marketing or horse biology or some other another topic completely unrelated to any other class you enrolled in.

In 2012, the Hewlett Foundation sponsored a contest to get some of the best minds in the world of machine learning – a revealingly named subsection of AI – to design a programmatic way to automate, not the grading of multiple choice tests or the selection of free courses, but the grading of essays.

The foundation offered a $100,000 bounty for an algorithm that would grade as well as humans. And it was a success; or at least, the bounty was claimed. Not only is it possible to automate essay grading, researchers contended, robots do this just as well as human essay-graders do.

Robots grade more efficiently. Robots, unlike those pesky human English instructors and graduate students, remain non-unionized. They do not demand a living wage or health care benefits.

A computer can grade 16,000 SAT essays in 20 seconds, I've heard cited, and if teachers don't have to worry about reading students' written work they can assign more of it. They can also have more – massively more – students in their classes. Hundreds of thousands more even.

Not everyone is sold on the idea that robot graders are the future. Many critics argue that it's actually pretty easy to fool the software. MIT's Les Perelman, for example, has written a piece of software in response called the Basic Automatic B.S. Essay Language Generator (or Babel) designed to auto-generate essays that can fool the robot graders. Fooling them can happen because robots don't "read" the way we do. They do things like assess word frequency, word placement, word pairing, word length, sentence length, use of conjunctions, and punctuation. They award a grade based in the scores that similar essays have received.

When you argue that automated essay-grading software functions about as good as a human grader, you've revealed something else too, as writing professor Alex Reid has argued: "If computers can read like people it's because we have trained people to read like computers."

Let's look closely at the human graders that these robots in the Hewlett

Foundation competition were compared to, for example. The major testing companies hire a range of people to grade essays for them. You'll often find "help wanted" ads on Craigslist for these sorts of positions. Sometimes you'll see them advertised as one of those promised "work from home" jobs.

From Todd Farley's book *Making the Grades: My Misadventures in the Standardized Testing Industry*"

"From my first day in the standardized testing industry (October 1994) until my last day (March 2008), I have watched those assessments be scored with rules that are alternately ambiguous, arbitrary, superficial, and bizarre. That has consistently proven to be the result of trying to establish scoring systems to assess 60,000 (or 100,000 or 10,000) student responses in some standardized way. Maybe one teacher scoring the tests of his or her own 30 students can use a rubric that differentiates rhetorically (a 3 showing 'complete understanding,' a 2 showing 'partial understanding,' and a 1 showing 'incomplete understanding'), but such a rubric simply never works on a project where the 10 or 20 scorers all have different ideas of what 'complete' or 'partial' means.

... I have watched the open-ended questions on large-scale assessments be scored by temporary employees who could be described as uninterested or unintelligent, apathetic or unemployable.

That, I'm afraid, is the dirty little secret of the standardized testing industry: The people hired to read and score student responses to standardized tests are, for the most part, people who can't get jobs elsewhere."

What might this tell us about the labor – its perceived value, its real value – that goes into the multibillion-dollar assessment industry? What might this tell us about the impetus behind its automation? What does this tell us, more broadly, about the everyday labor that goes into grading?

Of course, those hired to grade standardized tests aren't "the everyday." They don't have a personal relationship with the students they're grading. These graders are given a fairly strict rubric to follow – a rubric that computers, no surprise, follow with more precision. Human graders are discouraged from recognizing "creative" expression. Robot graders have no idea what "creative expression" even means.

But what does it mean to tell our students that we're actually not going to read their papers, but we're going to scan them and a computer will analyze them instead? What happens when we encourage students to express themselves in such a way that appeases the robot essay graders rather than a human audience? What happens when we discourage creative expression and instead encourage responsiveness to an algorithm?

Robot graders raise all sorts of questions about thinking machines and thinking humans, about self-expression and creativity, about the purpose of writing, the purpose of writing assignments, the purpose of education, the ethics of education technology, and the work that robots are being trained to do in education.

This isn't just about writing assessment, of course. There's the Math Emporium at Virginia Tech where some 8000 students take introductory math in a computer-based class with no professors. There are tutors, but that's academic labor of a very different sort.

What happens, in these settings, to pedagogy? What happens to research? What are the implications for instructors? What are the implications for students? What are the implications of automating the teaching and learning process? Why do we want the messy and open-ended process of inquiry standardized, scaled, or automated? What sort of society will this engineer? What will all of this artificial intelligence prompt us to do about human intelligence? What will it drive us to do about human relationships?

In 1962, Raymond Callahan published *Education and the Cult of Efficiency*, a rather dry book but an important one, an examination of the early twentieth century obsession to make schools run more like businesses, to bring "scientific management" or Taylorism to education. As Callahan makes clear, the process wasn't really about "science" or about "learning." Instead, when it came to the political pressures to "fix education," those charged with making schools operate more efficiently were found to "devote their attention to applying the scientific method to the financial and mechanical aspects of education."

A few years later, Jacques Ellul published *The Technological Society* in which he too identified efficiency as the all-encompassing, dominant force in our technological age. "The human brain must be made to conform to the much more advanced brain of the machine," he wrote. "And education will no longer be an unpredictable and exciting adventure in human enlightenment but an exercise in conformity and an apprenticeship to whatever gadgetry is useful in a technical world."

What "use" will our technical world have for us, for our students?

One more literary reference, one different from *Rossum's Universal Robots* and from *The Matrix*, one where the machines do not destroy their human creators. This comes from Isaac Asimov, who over the course of several short stories laid out a series of "Laws of Robotics:"

RULE 1: A ROBOT MAY NOT INJURE A HUMAN BEING, OR THROUGH INACTION, ALLOW A HUMAN BEING TO COME TO HARM.

RULE 2: A ROBOT MUST OBEY THE ORDERS GIVEN TO IT BY HUMAN BEINGS, EXCEPT WHERE SUCH ORDERS WOULD

CONFLICT WITH THE FIRST LAW.

RULE 3: A ROBOT MUST PROTECT ITS OWN EXISTENCE AS LONG AS SUCH PROTECTION DOES NOT CONFLICT WITH THE FIRST AND SECOND LAWS.

ZEROETH: A ROBOT MAY NOT HARM HUMANITY, OR BY INACTION, ALLOW HUMANITY TO COME TO HARM.

We have no laws of "ed-tech robotics." We rarely ask, "What are ethical implications of educational technologies?" Mostly, we want to know "will this raise test scores?" "Will this raise graduation rates?" We rarely ask, "Are we building and adopting tools that might harm us? That might destroy our humanity?"

That frames things in some nice science fiction hyperbole, I suppose, and elevates education technology to the level of "the survival of the human race" and the long-running battle of human versus machine. Perhaps hyperbole is too easy to dismiss. But when we raise questions about ethics and ed-tech robotics, they are questions about our humanity, about the future of our humanity. Indeed humanity and learning are deeply intertwined. They are intertwined with love, not with algorithms.

I'm not sure we need to devise laws of ed-tech robotics. Please do not invite me to the working group or weekend hackathon for that. But I do think we need to deliberate far more vigorously about the ethics and the consequences of the technologies we are adopting.

It's clear that building teaching machines has been a goal in the past. But that doesn't mean that doing so successfully counts as "progress." What is our vision for the future? Either we decide what these new technologies mean for us – what our ethical approach to technology will be – or someone else will. And sadly, it'll probably be someone whose studies were not grounded in the humanities.

This talk was delivered at Berkeley City College to kick off #BCCAgora, an event about outsourcing, adjunct labor, and higher education culture. The original transcript is available on Hack Education at http://hackeducation.com/2014/05/10/robots-and-education-labor/

WORKS CITED

Isaac Asimov, "Runaround." *Astounding Science Fiction*, March 1942.

Erik Brynjolfsson and Andrew McAfee, *Race Against the Machine: How the Digital Revolution is Accelerating Innovation, Driving Productivity, and Irreversibly Transforming Employment and the Economy*. Digital Frontier Press. 2011.

Raymond Callahan, *Education and the Cult of Efficiency*. University of Chicago Press, 1962.

Karel Čapek, *Rossum's Universal Robots*. Penguin Classics. 1920.

Jacques Ellul, *The Technological Society*. Vintage Books, 1964.

Todd Farley, *Making the Grades: My Misadventures in the Standardized Testing Industry*. Berrett-Koehler Publishers, 2009.

Ken Fisher, "'Negropodamus' disses Internet of Things, predicts knowledge pills," *Ars Technica*. March 18, 2014.

Kevin Kelly, "Better Than Human: Why Robots Will – And Must – Take Our Jobs." *Wired*. December 2012. http://www.wired.com/2012/12/ff-robots-will-take-our-jobs/all/

Alex Reid, "Robot Graders, New Aesthetic, and the End of the Close Reading Industry." April 18, 2012. http://alex-reid.net/2012/04/robot-graders-new-aesthetic-and-the-end-of-the-close-reading-industry.html

B. F. Skinner, *The Technology of Teaching*. Copley Publishing Group. 1968.

7 MOVING FROM "OPEN" TO JUSTICE

This is one of my most popular tweets:

Openwashing: n., having an appearance of open-source and open-licensing for marketing purposes, while continuing proprietary practices.

It hasn't gone viral by any means. But the two-and-a-half-year-old observation is resurfaced and retweeted pretty regularly.

I think the tweet resonated in part because we readily understand what "openwashing" means through what we know about the word's antecedents: "greenwashing," "pinkwashing," "whitewashing." We recognize with these terms that industry forces are quick to wrap themselves in language and imagery in the hopes it makes them appear more palatable, more friendly, more progressive. More "green," for example. More "open."

My tweet also gets at some of the frustrations that many of us experience when we see the word "open" used to describe things we feel are not "open" at all. It's a reflection of the ongoing challenges – conflicts even – that any "open" movement faces both internally and externally, as to what exactly is meant when that word is used.

And that's the thing. The definition and designation of "open" is fraught. Incredibly so. Even among those of us who consider ourselves advocates for openness in some form or another, we still scrap over which what counts as really truly "open."

In fairness, my tweet about "openwashing" wasn't aimed at the debates about AGPL3 or Attribution-Non Commercial. It was a subtweet, if you will, a reference to the learning management system Blackboard's acquisition of Moodlerooms and Netspot, two companies that help provide support and deployment services for schools that use the open-source LMS

Moodle. "Ours is no mere dalliance with open source," the company said at the time. "Openwashing," I muttered under my breath, right before I tweeted.

Blackboard is hardly alone here. In education technology – my field, that is – I can list for you any number of examples of companies and organizations that have attached that word "open" to their products and services: OpenClass, an learning management system built by Pearson, the largest education company in the world and one of the largest publishers of proprietary textbooks. I don't know what "open" refers to there in OpenClass. The Open Education Alliance, an industry group founded by the online education startup Udacity. I don't know what "open" refers to there in the Open Education Alliance. The startup Open English, an online English-language learning site and one of the most highly funded startups in the last few years. I don't know what "open" refers to there in Open English.

All these append "open" to a name without really even trying to append "openness," let alone embrace "openness," to their practices or mission. Whatever "openness" means.

Let me repeat that, because it's important: *whatever "openness" means.*

Does "open" mean openly licensed content or code? And, again, which license is really "open"? Does "open" mean "made public"? Does "open" mean shared? Does "open" mean "accessible"? Accessible how? To whom? Does "open" mean editable? "Forkable"? Negotiable? Does "open" mean "free"? Does "open" mean "open-ended"? Does "open" mean "transparent"? Does "open" mean "open-minded"? "Open" to new ideas and to intellectual exchange? "Open" to interpretation? Does "open" mean open to participation and to participation by everyone equally? Open doors? Open opportunity? Open to suggestion? Or does it mean "open for business"?

That's the problem. "Open" means all those things. And on one hand, multivalence is good. Having many meanings, many interpretations can be a strength. On the other hand, it's a weakness when the term becomes so widely applied that it is rendered meaningless. I worry often that that's what we're faced with. "Open" has ended up being a bit like Supreme Court Justice Potter Stewart's famous assertion that "I know [obscenity] when I see it." That is, we hear a lot of "I know 'open' when I see it" sorts of claims. If those of us who work within "open" efforts cannot always agree on what that adjective means, how do we expect others to? Should we expect others to?

I've actually come to believe, in the two plus years since I tweeted my critique of "openwashing," that the answer here isn't actually a clearer definition of "open." The answer isn't more fights for a more rigid adherence to a particular license.

I think the answer is more transparency about and more urgency in our politics. I think, in fact, the answer *is* politics.

We act at our peril as if "open" is politically neutral, let alone politically good or progressive. Indeed, we sometimes use the word to stand in place of a politics of participatory democracy. We presume that, because something is "open" that it necessarily contains all the conditions for equality or freedom or justice. We use "open" as though it is free of ideology, ignoring how much "openness," particularly as it's used by technologists, is closely intertwined with "meritocracy" – this notion, a false one, that "open" wipes away inequalities, institutions, biases, history, that "open" "levels the playing field."

If we believe in equality, if we believe in participatory democracy and participatory culture, if we believe in people and progressive social change, if we believe in sustainability in all its environmental and economic and psychological manifestations, then we need to do better than slap that adjective "open" onto our projects and act as though that's sufficient or – and this is hard, I know – even sound.

I want to make an argument here today that we need to be more explicit about these politics. We can't pretend like "open" is going to do that work for us. In fact, we need to recognize: it might not be doing that work at all.

In particular, I want to examine at how "open" is invoked around education data, and I want to suggest that instead of a push for more "open data" in education, we need to instead – this is a phrase I am borrowing from Utah Valley University researcher Jeffrey Alan Johnson – to push for "information justice."

When we talk about "opening" education data, I'd argue that we always have to tread very carefully. Education data lives in this tricky and powerful in-between space of public and private; it is both-and. That is, it is often data generated at and collected by publicly funded institutions. It is also deeply personal data, if not legally protected private data. Furthermore, the data that is collected often fulfills institutional needs, rather than learners'. That collection is often compelled, for reasons that might be progressive, and for politics that might not be.

And now, thanks to the proliferation of educational technologies, the sorts of data and the compulsions to collect it are increasing.

The push for more education data collection is not new. Not remotely. The National Center for Education Statistics has existed since 1867, when Congress passed legislation providing "That there shall be established at the City of Washington, a department of education, for the purpose of collecting such statistics and facts as shall show the condition and progress of education in the several States and Territories, and of diffusing such information respecting the organization and management of schools and school systems, and methods of teaching, as shall aid the people of the

66

United States in the establishment and maintenance of efficient school systems, and otherwise promote the cause of education throughout the country." Over a hundred years before there was a Department of Education, that is, the federal government was collecting education data.

As such local, state, and federal governments, along with educational institutions themselves have long tracked "data" about students. Since the advent of No Child Left Behind under George W. Bush, data collection has become part of a larger disciplinary effort, to identify and punish "failing schools." And under Barack Obama's No Child Left Behind policy, the data collection has only continued, an effort that dovetails quite nicely with schools' increasing adoption of computer technologies and, as such, students' increasing generation of "data exhaust."

The current administration is interested in more than just data at the school, district, and state level. It's actively promoting the collection and analysis of student at the individual level, arguing that if we just have more data – if we "open up" the classroom, the software, the databases, the educational practices – that we will unlock the secrets of how every student learns. We can then build software that caters to that, something that will make learning more efficient and more personalized. Or that's the argument at least. We should remember that this is mostly speculative. And we should recognize here that words like "personalization" function much like "open." That is, they sound great in press releases, but they should prompt us to ask more questions rather than assume that they're necessarily good.

In 2012, the Department of Education announced the Education Data Initiative, part of the larger Open Data Initiative that in its words will "'liberate' government data and voluntarily-contributed non-government data as fuel to spur entrepreneurship, create value, and create jobs while improving educational outcomes for students." That is, "open education data" isn't simply about citizens reviewing the success or failure or funding or outcomes of schools. It's not about shifting power, thanks to "openness," from the federal government – those darn data hoarders – to the people, to communities, to teachers, parents, or students. Nope.

It is however a shift in power.

The push to "open" more education data has happened at the state level too. With a nod from the Council of Chief State School Officers (that is, an organization of state superintendents of education which has also been a major strategic proponent of the recent Common Core State Standards), and funded with $100 million from the Carnegie Corporation and Gates Foundation, the Shared Learning Collaborative – later rebranded to inBloom – launched in 2011, promising to create a massive warehouse of student data that would be "open" to third-party developers.

The infrastructure would be open-source, replacing what is, in so many cases, an ailing infrastructure of often proprietary databases, applications, and systems that many school districts work with to manage students' records.

And here, immediately, we can see the some of the problems with "open." Because the code for InBloom was meant to be open source, it does offer some leverage against the proprietary infrastructure that most schools are saddled with: Pearson PowerSchool or eScholar for starters. Ideally, thanks open source, any school could install the inBloom codebase and be free of the inBloom organization and all its attachments to News Corp (that's who wrote a great deal of the code), to the Gates Foundation (that's who funded the project), and so on.

But then what? Open source doesn't actually get us out of the conundrum that is education data collection. Open source doesn't opt you out of reporting mandates, for example. Indeed, "open" might put us farther into the weeds.

InBloom's data specification included hundreds of data points about students – enough to make parents and privacy groups balk about what exactly is being collected and shared and why. It probably didn't help that some of the development work was done by Wireless Generation, a company that had been acquired by News Corporation, right in the middle of that company's phone hacking scandal. And it probably didn't help when those in education technology make ridiculously triumphant claims about all the data-mining they plan to do.

Take, for example, the CEO of Knewton, which is a company that promises to take student data and provide "adaptive" pathways through textbook lessons, who pronounced that "We literally know everything about what you know and how you learn best, everything." Knewton boasts that it gathers millions of data points on millions of children each day. He calls education "the world's most data-mineable industry by far." "We have five orders of magnitude more data about you than Google has," the Knewton CEO said at a Department of Education "Datapalooza" event. "We literally have more data about our students than any company has about anybody else about anything, and it's not even close."

The argument – espoused by the Department of Education, handily doing the bidding of administration and administrative fetishes for data as well as the bidding of education technology companies like Knewton and inBloom and others – is that more data works in the service of "better education," that the problem that schools have long faced stem, in part, from a failure to collect and make use of data.

Data is kept in silos – in spreadsheets, in student information systems, in handwritten grade books – so the story goes (I believe that story), and therefore there hasn't been a way to understand each child (that's bullshit), to see a full data profile of a particular student, let alone create algorithms and software best suited to move that student through school.

Again, the collection of education data isn't new. Indeed, inBloom used a data model that was based in part upon SIF, the schools interoperability framework, a specification that is over a decade old. What was new here was the push to have this data be "open" more easily to third party developers and not simply to the one company that won the contract for the student information system.

But to challenge inBloom and others in education technology who are interested in educational data collection and data-mining, we need to do more than raise red flags about privacy. That's been the loudest complaint. A parent-led effort did just that, successfully organizing protests in the states and districts that were piloting the inBloom technology. One by one, these customers backed out. Louisiana. Colorado. New York. Illinois. By April of this year, inBloom had no customers left, and it announced that it was closing its doors. $100 million. For what it's worth, some of the code is available on Github.

But I want to raise more questions about the data itself. Data is not neutral. Data – its collection, storage, retrieval, usage – is not neutral. There can be, as Jeffrey Alan Johnson argues, "injustices embedded in the data itself," and when we "open data," it does not necessarily ameliorate these. In fact, open data might serve to re-inscribe these, to reinforce privilege in no small part because data, open or not, is often designed around meeting the needs around businesses and institutions and not around meeting the needs of citizens, or in this case students.

What "counts" as education data? Let's start there. What do schools collect?

As I said earlier, the inBloom data spec included hundreds of data points. A small sampling: Academic Honors, Attendance Type, Behavior Incident Type, Career Pathway, Disability Type, Disciplinary Action, Grade Point Average, Incident Location, Personal Information Verification Type, Reason for Restraint, Eligibility for Free or Reduced School Lunch, Special Accommodation, Student Characteristic, Weapon Type.

I think it's clear, as I list these, that the moments when students generate "education data" are historically moments when they come into contact with the school and more broadly the school and the state as a disciplinary system. We need to think more critically, more carefully about what it means to open up this data – data that is often mandated by the state to be collected – to others, to businesses. Again, is "open data" about liberating data, as the Department of Education suggests, "to spur entrepreneurship, create value, and create jobs while improving educational outcomes for students"?

As Johnson argues, "the opening of data can function as a tool of disciplinary power. Open data enhances the capacity of disciplinary systems" – and school certainly functions as one of those – "to observe and evaluate institutions' and individuals' conformity to norms that become the core values and assumptions of the institutional system whether or not they reflect the circumstances of those institutions and individuals."

Did you speak out of turn in class? Are you a child of an illegal immigrant? Did you get written up for wearing a halter top? Are you pregnant? Did you miss school? Why?

What classes did you take? What grades did you make? Why?

(Is the answer to "why" a data point? And – here's the rub – is that "data point" ever connected to an ethics of care or a sense of social justice?)

Education data often highlights the ways in which we view students as objects not as subjects of their own learning. I'll repeat my refrain: education data is not neutral. Opening education data does not necessarily benefit students or schools or communities; it does not benefit all students, all schools, all communities equally. Open source education data warehouses are not neutral. And similarly, the source code does not benefit students equally.

If we are to move, as Johnson suggests we do, from "open data" to "information justice," we cannot depend on technology alone. Nor can we rely on that word "open" to serve as the metric by which we evaluate our practices and policies. This isn't an argument for "closed" or "proprietary" systems. Not by any stretch. It's an argument for building capacity and agency. We need to consider, for example, what data looks like in communities' hands, in students' hands, what information students would want to collect on themselves, for themselves, who they would want to share it with and why. And in doing so, we need to recognize the messiness of our learning, of our data and not normalize that for the sake of analysis, not open it for the sake of control.

Read this way, "openwashing" might signal something else other than a misused marketing term.

What happens when something is "open" in all the ways that open education and open source and open data advocates would approve. All the right open licenses. All the right levels of accessibility. All the right nods from all the right powerful players within "open." And yet, the project is still not equitable.

What if, in fact, it's making it worse.

What are we going to do when and if we recognize that "open" is not enough? I hope, that we recognize that what we need in turn is social justice. We need politics, not simply a license. We need politics, not simply technology solutions. We need an ethics of care, of justice, not simply an assumption that "open" can do the work of those things for us.

This keynote was delivered at OpenCon on November 16, 2014 in Washington, DC. The original transcript can be found on Hack Education at http://www.hackeducation.com/2014/11/16/from-open-to-justice/

WORKS CITED

Jose Ferreira, "Knewton at Education Datapalooza." http://youtu.be/Lr7Z7ysDluQ

Jeffrey Alan Johnson. "From Open Data to Information Justice." Annual Conference of the Midwest Political Science Association. April 13, 2013. Chicago, Illinois.

8 MEN EXPLAIN TECHNOLOGY TO ME: ON GENDER, ED-TECH, AND THE REFUSAL TO BE SILENT

This is (I think) the last public talk I will give this year. It has been the most difficult one to prepare.

I put a lot of myself – my ideas and anecdotes from my life – into my talks. But when asked to speak to you today about gender and educational technology, I have found myself at a bit of a loss as to how much of "me" I wanted to include here, and how much of others' experiences I felt comfortable invoking as well.

I have lots to say, don't get me wrong. I have personal experiences. And I have a Women's Studies degree, dammit! But to say something publicly – out loud, in person or online, to commit these thoughts to writing, any of it – is a little intimidating at this very moment, particularly as I can still see the fallout from Gamergate wreak havoc on people's lives. I consider myself pretty damn fierce and fearless. But I've sat staring at a blinking cursor trying to figure out what to say and, I admit, a little apprehensive about potential reactions, particularly if I call out -isms and/or name names.

But I know I have to come right out and say it, because very few people in education technology will: there's a problem with computer technology. Culturally. Ideologically. There's a problem with the Internet. Largely designed by men *from* the developed world, it is built *for* men of the developed world. Men of science. Men of industry. Military men. Venture capitalists. Despite all the hype and hope about revolution and access and opportunity that these new technologies will provide us, they do not negate hierarchy, history, privilege, power. They reflect those. They channel them. They concentrate them, in new ways and in old.

Harassment – of women, people of color, and other marginalized groups – is pervasive online. It's a reflection of offline harassment, to be sure. But there are mechanics of the Internet – its architecture, affordances, infrastructure, its culture – that can alter, even exacerbate what that harassment looks like and how it is experienced.

For advocates of education technology, this is a bitter pill to swallow: Internet technologies are not simply generative or supportive; they can be destructive. But this, all of this is an ed-tech issue. It is a technology issue. It is an education issue. It a societal issue. It is a political issue. We cannot ignore it. But that's precisely what most people in ed-tech seem to do.

In my head, I hear that voice, that sneering response from certain corners of the Internet: "Well, that's just your opinion, lady."

OK. Sure. All my work conceivably falls under the heading "opinion." My analysis (that's the term I prefer) is however grounded in research and in observation. Often I include personal experience narratives too – perhaps as a way to position myself as an authority in a field in which I am neither formally degreed nor formally employed.

In planning my talk today, specifically when thinking about what I have to say about gender and ed-tech, that "opinion" feels pretty vulnerable. Or rather, I feel pretty vulnerable. It's not an intellectual vulnerability. Frankly, I feel some of that all the time. Like: what if this essay is dumb or wrong? What if the thing I think is a brilliant observation is just a mediocre version of what some smarter person wrote last week, last year, a decade ago, and so on. "Imposter syndrome," I suppose.

I'm talking here about a different, heightened sort of vulnerability – not intellectual but psychological and physical. That is, my work comes from a body – my body, a marked body. Gendered and therefore not objective. Always subjective. Always opinion.

Gendered. This is the lens through which I write. It is how I experience the world. White cis heterosexual American female.

It is how I experience the Internet.

There's that very famous *New Yorker* cartoon: "On the Internet, nobody knows you're a dog." The cartoon was first published in 1993 – fairly interesting, I think, because it shows that by the early 1990s, the Internet had achieved if not a popular appeal, then enough of one that those who read the *New Yorker* could chuckle about the reference. The cartoon demonstrates too this sense that we have long had that the Internet offers privacy and anonymity, that we can experiment with identities online in ways that are severed from our bodies, from our material selves and that, potentially at least, the Internet can allow online participation for those denied it offline.

Perhaps, yes.

But sometimes when folks on the Internet discover "you're a dog," they do everything in their power to put you back in your place, to remind you of your body. To punish you for being there. To hurt you. To destroy you. Online and offline.

The following sentence sounds so weird, I realize, when I say it out loud: I have received death threats. I write about education technology; I write online for a living. And I've had people respond to my work by saying they wanted to kill me, they wanted to see me die. I've had death threats, rape threats – subtle and overt. Most often what I get are the type my friend Tressie McMillan Cottom describes as "Who the fuck do you think you are?" comments. But I've been threatened. I've been told to shut up. Some harassment is sporadic; some serial. In response, I've taken the comments off my blog. The harassment continues via email. It happens on platforms like Twitter and Facebook and Google+. I block, I delete, I flag as spam. It's up to me to monitor and respond to this. I have filed complaints and reports on these social media platforms, but rarely is anything done. It becomes part of the "work" *I* have to do in order to do *my* work online.

When I tell people that these are my experiences, they often respond, "Are the threats real?" That's a question that is hard to answer. No, nobody has come to my door. But yes, they are real. I experience them as real. Even if nobody physically hurts me, these threats take a very material toll on me. They affect my work, my mental health, my physical health, my relationship with my partner, my life.

For a long time, I wondered what it was about my work, about me that was really so controversial. I hear that too. If I could just "soften it up." "Say nice things every once in a while." "Smile." And true, my work is critical, sometimes bitingly, angrily so.

But I know that the threats and the harassment are not, at their core, about the content of my blog posts or the substance of my arguments. They're not about tech or ed-tech or "ethics in video game journalism." The threats come because I am, quite simply, a woman who expresses an opinion on the Internet. They come because I am a woman.

One of my favorite essays is by the writer Rebecca Solnit: "Men Explain Things to Me." She first wrote the essay in 2008 and since then the term "mansplaining" has become so popular – we use it often to describe the Internet version of men explaining things to women – that she published a whole book on the topic earlier this year.

"Mansplaining" is a microaggression, a practice of undermining women's intelligence, our contributions, our voice, our experiences, our knowledge, our expertise; and frankly once these pile up, these mansplaining microaggressions, they undermine women's feelings of self-worth. Women then decide not to speak.

Let me quote Solnit (my apologies, at length):

...I was in Berlin giving a talk when the Marxist writer Tariq Ali invited me out to a dinner that included a male writer and translator and three women a little younger than me who would remain deferential and mostly silent throughout the dinner. Tariq was great. Perhaps the translator was peeved that I insisted on playing a modest role in the conversation, but when I said something about how Women Strike for Peace, the extraordinary, little-known antinuclear and antiwar group founded in 1961, helped bring down the communist-hunting House Committee on Un-American Activities, HUAC, Mr. Very Important II sneered at me. HUAC, he insisted, didn't exist by the early 1960s and, anyway, no women's group played such a role in HUAC's downfall. His scorn was so withering, his confidence so aggressive, that arguing with him seemed a scary exercise in futility and an invitation to more insult.

I think I was at nine books at that point, including one that drew from primary documents and interviews about Women Strike for Peace. But explaining men still assume I am, in some sort of obscene impregnation metaphor, an empty vessel to be filled with their wisdom and knowledge. A Freudian would claim to know what they have and I lack, but intelligence is not situated in the crotch—even if you can write one of Virginia Woolf's long mellifluous musical sentences about the subtle subjugation of women in the snow with your willie. Back in my hotel room, I Googled a bit and found that Eric Bentley in his definitive history of the House Committee on Un-American Activities credits Women Strike for Peace with "striking the crucial blow in the fall of HUAC's Bastille." In the early 1960s.

So I opened an essay for the *Nation* with this interchange, in part as a shout-out to one of the more unpleasant men who have explained things to me: Dude, if you're reading this, you're a carbuncle on the face of humanity and an obstacle to civilization. Feel the shame.

The battle with Men Who Explain Things has trampled down many women—of my generation, of the up-and-coming generation we need so badly, here and in Pakistan and Bolivia and Java, not to speak of the countless women who came before me and were not allowed into the laboratory, or the library, or the conversation, or the revolution, or even the category called human.

After all, Women Strike for Peace was founded by women who were tired of making the coffee and doing the typing and not having any voice or decision-making role in the antinuclear movement of the 1950s. Most women fight wars on two fronts, one for whatever the putative topic is and one simply for the right to speak, to have ideas, to be acknowledged to be in possession of facts and truths, to have value, to be a human being. Things have certainly gotten better, but this war won't end in my lifetime. I'm still fighting it, for myself certainly, but also for all those younger women who have something to say, in the hope that they will get to say it."

Thanks to feminism, to feminist pedagogy, we can recognize when incidents of mansplaining occurs in academia or in the classroom, right? We can see when a young woman has something terrifically smart to say – perhaps based on their research, their analysis, their personal experience – and a man will interrupt and interject and explain whatever the topic is more loudly, more forcefully, with all the assuredness and the "well, actually" that comes with male privilege.

I think – I hope – that as educators we try to elevate the marginalized voices in our classrooms. Online, we don't do that so well. The mansplaining can be overpowering.

I speak from experience. On Twitter, I have over 26,000 followers, most of whom follow me, I'd wager, because from time to time I say smart things about education technology. Yet regularly, men – strangers, typically, but not always – jump into my "@-mentions" to explain education technology to me. To explain open source licenses or open data or open education or MOOCs to me. Men explain learning management systems to me. Men explain the history of education technology to me. Men explain privacy and education data to me. Men explain venture capital funding of education startups to me. Men explain online harassment to me. Men explain blogging to me. Men explain, they explain, they explain.

It's exhausting. It's insidious. It doesn't quite elevate to the level of harassment, to be sure; but these microaggressions often mean that when harassment or threats do occur, women like me are already worn down. Yet this is all part of my experiences online. My experiences. Women's experiences. My friends' experiences.

I started to make a list of all the women I know who've experienced online harassment in the last year or so. Adria. Sarah. Another Sarah. A different Sarah. Brianna. Shanley. Suey. Tressie. Julie. Another Julie. Rose. Ariel. Anita. Kathy. Zoe. Amanda. Ashe. Catherine. Felicia. Mikki. Mia. Molly. Lauren. Jenn. A different Jen. Jessica. Jessie. Jess. Caroline. Katie. Sadie. Bridget. Alyssa. Lyndy. Rebecca. Roxane. I could go on, but I have to stop. I cannot breathe as I continue to say these names out loud.

I should be clear: for many of these women, the harassment has moved offline as well. They've been doxxed, for example – that is where your address and phone number and other identifiable information are posted online in forums like 4chan for the specific purpose to offline harassment.

Take the actress Felicia Day, who recently posted her thoughts about Gamergate, what's become an ongoing campaign of harassment against women in gaming.

"I have tried to retweet a few of the articles I've seen dissecting the issue in support, but personally I am terrified to be doxxed for even typing the words 'Gamer Gate'," she wrote.

"I have had stalkers and restraining orders issued in the past, I have had people show up on my doorstep when my personal information was HARD to get. To have my location revealed to the world would give a entry point for a few mentally ill people who have fixated on me, and allow them to show up and make good on the kind of threats I've received that make me paranoid to walk around a convention alone. I haven't been able to stomach the risk of being afraid to get out of my car in my own driveway because I've expressed an opinion that someone on the internet didn't agree with.

HOW SICK IS THAT?"

Almost instantly after she posted this to her Tumblr, she was doxxed. *Almost instantly*. That's how it increasingly works. Speak up online; have your offline world – that is, your physical safety – exposed, threatened.

For many women, myself included, our profession and our work demand we be online. We are writers and artists and journalists and actors and speakers and educators and students. We cannot *not* be online.

It's easy for some people to suggest, I think, that some of us are targeted because of our high(er) profile. And we are, I suppose, easier – or more recognizable at least – targets. Perhaps. But that's also beside the point. Because here's the thing that comes with being "Internet famous": as high(er)-profile Internet users, some of also have powerful connections to, say, staff at Twitter or Tumblr that elevate and prioritize our complaints, that shut down the accounts of our harassers more rapidly than "regular" users will ever experience.

And "regular users" do indeed experience online harassment.

The Pew Research Internet Project recently published the results from a survey on online harassment. Among the findings: "60% of Internet users said they had witnessed someone being called offensive names. 53% had seen efforts to purposefully embarrass someone. 25% had seen someone being physically threatened. 24% witnessed someone being harassed for a sustained period of time. 19% said they witnessed someone being sexually harassed. 18% said they had seen someone be stalked."

According to the Pew survey, 22% of all Internet users reported being harassed online. One in 5. About 55% of those said they had experienced the "less severe" forms; that means 45% said they had experienced the "more severe" forms, including serial harassment, sexual harassment, and stalking. Young women – those age 18 to 24, those we still label as "college age" – experience the most severe harassment online. "26% of these young women have been stalked online, and 25% were the target of online sexual harassment."

All this in the Pew survey is self-reported, I should note. So when Pew says something like, "Overall, men are somewhat more likely than women to experience at least one of the elements of online harassment, 44% vs. 37%," we should probably make it very clear, again, that the harassment that men and women receive online is different – in degree, in purpose, in results. A different organization. W.H.O.A. ("Working to Halt Online Abuse") has found that 73% of cyberstalking victims are women, for example. A University of Maryland research project created fake online accounts and set them into Internet chat rooms. "Accounts with feminine usernames incurred an average of 100 sexually explicit or threatening messages a day. Masculine names received 3.7."

Again I want to make the connection here to our offline bodies. An earlier Pew study found that "five percent of women who used the Internet said 'something happened online' that led them into 'physical danger.'" And as statistics about violence against women should remind us, this isn't simply a problem that stems from the Internet. From the World Health Organization: "Violence against women is widespread around the world. Recent figures indicate that 35% of women worldwide have experienced either intimate partner violence or non-partner sexual violence in their lifetime. ...Women who have been physically or sexually abused have higher rates of mental ill-health, unintended pregnancies, abortions and miscarriages than non-abused women. ... Increasingly in many conflicts, sexual violence is also used as a tactic of war."

We do not escape our material bodies online, as much as that New Yorker cartoon suggests we might.

In fact, I want to argue that online – computer technologies, Internet technologies – actually re-inscribe our material bodies, the power and the ideology of gender and race and sexual identity and national identity. Why? In part, because of who is making these tools.

News organizations have been pushing for several years for the major technology companies to release their diversity numbers – that is, the make-up of their workforce. In fact, many of these companies have fought attempts to publish their EEO (Equal Employment Opportunity) data. But this year, perhaps recognizing that they must at some point address the "pipeline issue" – how to get more women and people of color into STEM-related fields – some tech companies have released this data. And it's not pretty.

70% of Google's employees are male. 61% are white and 30% Asian. Of Google's "technical" employees. 83% are male. 60% of those are white and 34% are Asian.

70% of Apple's employees are male. 55% are white and 15% are Asian. 80% of Apple's "technical" employees are male.

69% of Facebook's employees are male. 57% are white and 34% are Asian. 85% of Facebook's "technical" employees are male.

70% of Twitter's employees are male. 59% are white and 29% are Asian. 90% of Twitter's "technical" employees are male.

So gee, I wonder why blocking violent harassers, reporting rape threats, banning sock-puppet accounts, and so on hasn't been a priority for Twitter.

And I wonder too: what do these demographics look like for education technology companies? What percentage of those building ed-tech software are men? What percentage is white? What percentage of ed-tech companies' engineers are men? How do these bodies shape what gets built? How do privileges, ideologies, expectations, values get hard-coded into ed-tech?

We tend to view the education profession as a female one. At the K-12 level, three-quarters of teachers are women, and over 80% are white. (It's worth noting that, this school year, for the first time, nonwhite students outnumber white students in public schools.) At the higher education level, 48% of college instructors are women; again, almost 80% are white. But it's a mistake to think that education is somehow "female-dominated," that women are well-represented in leadership or decision-making roles, or that women in education do not experience work-related harassment or discriminatory treatment. And once we add technology to the picture, I daresay it gets worse.

What percentage of education technologists are men? What percentage of "education technology leaders" are men? What percentage of education technology consultants? What percentage of those on the education technology speaking circuit? What percentage of education CIOs and CTOs; what percentage of ed-tech CEOs?

Again: How do these bodies – in turn, their privileges, ideologies, expectations, values – influence our education technologies?

So I'm speaking to a group of educators and students here. I'm probably supposed to say something about what we can do, right? What we can do to resist that hard-coding. What we can do to subvert that hard-coding. What we can do to make technologies that our students – all our students, all of us – can wield. What we can do to make sure that when we say "your assignment involves the Internet" that we haven't triggered half the class with fears of abuse, harassment, exposure, rape, death.

The answer can't simply be to tell women to not use their real name online. If part of the argument for participating in the open Web is that students and educators are building a digital portfolio, are building a professional network, are contributing to scholarship, then we have to really think about whether or not promoting pseudonyms is a sufficient or an equitable solution.

The answer can't be simply be "don't blog on the open Web." Or "keep everything inside the 'safety' of the walled garden, the learning management system." If nothing else, this presumes that what happens inside siloed, online spaces is necessarily "safe." I've seen plenty of horrible behavior on closed forums, for example, from professors and students alike. I've seen heavy-handed moderation, where marginalized voices find their input is deleted. I've seen zero moderation, where marginalized voices are mobbed.

The answer can't simply be "just don't read the comments." I would say that it might be worth rethinking "comments" on student blogs altogether – or at least questioning the expectation that students host them, moderate them, respond to them. See, if we give students the opportunity to "own their own domain," to have their own websites, their own space on the Web, we really shouldn't require them to let anyone that can create a user account into that space. It's perfectly acceptable to say to someone who wants to comment on a blog post, "Respond on your own site. Link to me. But I am under no obligation to host your thoughts in my domain."

That starts to hint at what I think the answer here to this question about the unpleasantness, by design, of technology. It starts to get at what any sort of "solution" or "alternative" has to look like: it has to be both social and technical. If, as I've argued, the current shape of education technologies has been shaped by certain ideologies and certain bodies, we should recognize that we aren't stuck with those. We don't have to "do" tech as it's been done. We can design differently. We can design around. We can use differently. We can use around.

One interesting example of this dual approach that combines both social and technical – outside the realm of ed-tech, I recognize – is the BlockBot. Having grown weary of Twitter's refusal to address the ways in which its platform is utilized to harass people, a group of feminist developers wrote the BlockBot, an application that when you install it, lets you block, en masse, a large list of Twitter accounts that are known for being serial harassers. That list of blocked accounts is updated and maintained collaboratively.

That gets, just a bit, at what I think we can do in order to make education technology habitable, sustainable, and healthy. We have to rethink the technology. And not simply as some nostalgia for a "Web we lost," for example, but as a move forward to a Web we've yet to ever see, one that is inclusive and equitable. Perhaps education needs reminding of this: we don't have to adopt tools that serve business goals or administrative purposes, particularly when they are to the detriment of scholarship and/or student agency – technologies that surveil and control and restrict, for example, under the guise of "safety" – that gets trotted out from time to time, but that have never ever been about students' needs at all. We don't have to accept that technology must extract value from us. We don't have to accept that technology puts us at risk. We don't have to accept that the architecture, the infrastructure of these tools makes it easy for harassment to occur without any consequences. We can build different and better technologies. And we can build them with and for communities, communities of scholars and communities of learners. We don't have to be paternalistic as we do so. We don't have to "protect students from the Internet" and rehash all the arguments about stranger danger and predators and pedophiles from the 1990s. But we should recognize that if we want education to be online, if we want education to be immersed in technologies, information, and networks, that we can't really throw students out there alone. We need to be braver and more compassionate and we need to build that into ed-tech. Like Blockbot, this should be a collaborative effort, one that blends our cultural values with the technology that we ourselves design and build.

Because here's the thing. The answer to all of this – to harassment online, to the male domination of the technology industry – is not inaction. And it is not silence. That is after all, as Rebecca Solnit reminds us, one of the goals of mansplaining: to get us to cower, to hesitate, to doubt ourselves and our stories and our needs, to step back, to shut up.

I'll repeat: the answer is not silence.

I think the most important cautionary tale, if you will, about gender and equity and silence comes not from Gamergate but from the revelations last month about Canadian radio celebrity Jian Ghomeshi. Ghomeshi, the host of a popular radio program, was suddenly fired by the CBC, and allegations quickly emerged of numerous violent sexual assaults. Ghomeshi, for his part, said this involved spurned ex-lovers and he was being punished for what was, in his words, consensual BDSM. The women – and there are over 8 accusers now – say otherwise. It was not consensual. It was assault.

But it isn't just these brave women who've come forward. A large number of members of the Canadian media, of the Vancouver and Toronto music scenes have spoken out too, confessing "they knew about Jian." They knew. There was talk. Chatter. Warnings. One woman wrote a piece explaining carefully that when people asked "do you know about Jian," the question didn't imply "do you know Jian Ghomeshi, popular radio host?" It meant "do *you* know." "Just be careful. He's weird with woman," a male friend had warned her when she first joined "the scene." And she writes,

"Warned by this, I kept my distance and just watched. I saw the way he moved towards women, introduced himself, and pushed his way into their space. ... Nothing you'd call a crime, not quite. Nothing you could name. Just a sense, all the little things that added up to say – this isn't safe. This person is not safe.

Boundary issues, call 'em, and they were persistent. I saw it on other occasions after that, though only a few – other parties, where I'd lean my head against another woman's so that we could exchange our warnings in the night. Through these other women I started to hear stories, filtering through in little bites: it felt like everyone had a friend with a story. A friend who was hurt or leered at. A friend who had been uncomfortable, cornered or afraid.

But how could you say that, in a way that would ever be believed? How would you describe that for the world, in a way that the world would ever believe?

So instead, you start to turn to the women around you, and you say: 'do you know about Jian?'

And you watch them nod, and pass it on."

That's how networks work, isn't it. You exchange important information. You try to build community and keep that community safe. But we can see in this anecdote how much access to that network matters. Networks offer protection. If you weren't part of the right network, perhaps you didn't hear the whispered warnings. Or perhaps you were part of an adjacent network, a network of powerful media people that "knew about Jian" but chose not to say anything or do anything publicly.

It's not a perfect analogy to ed-tech, by any means. But I want to draw the comparison because I feel like the stakes are very high. We have to think about the networks we are building and we are using. How do they reflect information and power? Who do they protect? Who do they put at risk?

We can't sit back and let harassment and abuse go on. We can't ignore it, or pretend that it doesn't exist or that, because it's online it isn't real.

We can't retreat behind walls. We women know that violence happens there too, of course. Being out in the public space – and these days, that means being on the Internet – is how we shed light, is how we give voice, and is how we fully participate in civic life.

Yes, we can whisper tips to our friends, our colleagues, our students. We can work quietly to resist. We can build alternative networks and alternative education technologies. But we cannot – ed-tech cannot – be silent.

This talk was delivered at the University of Mary Washington and to the University of Regina on November 18, 2014. The original transcript is available at http://www.hackeducation.com/2014/11/18/gender-and-ed-tech/

WORKS CITED

Felicia Day, "The Only Thing I Have to Say About Gamer Gate." November 2014. http://thisfeliciaday.tumblr.com/post/100700417809/the-only-thing-i-have-to-say-about-gamer-gate

Tressie McMillan Cottom, "'Who The Fuck Do You Think You Are?' Academic Engagement, Microcelebrity, and Digital Sociology from the Far Left of the Matrix of Domination."

http://www.academia.edu/7278027/_Who_Do_You_Think_You_Are_Ac
ademic_Engagement_Microcelebrity_and_Digital_Sociology_from_the_Far
_Left_of_the_Matrix_of_Domination

Melissa Martin, "Do You Know About Jian."
http://www.nothinginwinnipeg.com/2014/10/do-you-know-about-jian/

Pew Research Center, "Online Harassment." October 22, 2014
http://www.pewinternet.org/2014/10/22/online-harassment/

Rebecca Solnit, *Men Explain Things to Me.* Haymarket Books, 2014.

III. FROM MONSTERS TO THE MARVELOUS

9 ED-TECH'S MONSTERS

On Monday, on our way up here to Coventry, we – that is, my mum, my boyfriend, and I – stopped at Bletchley Park, the site of the British government's Code and Cypher School during the Second World War and the current location of the National Museum of Computing.

When we were planning our trip, I mentioned to my mum that I wanted to stop at Bletchley Park, and she said "Oh! Your grandfather did some work there" – a bit of family history I'd like to have known, as someone who now writes about computers for a living, but a bit of family history that I hadn't ever considered until that moment. It makes sense. During the war my grandfather was the station commander at Chain Home Low, an early warning radar base, and later became Air Officer Commanding-in-Chief at Signals Command. Although he was knighted for his work on the development of radar, I'm not sure how much he really talked about that work with the family. My granny said that during the war she never actually knew what he did. She never asked. And he passed away before many of his stories were de-classified.

I am, as some of you know, a folklorist by academic training. Not an instructional designer. Not an education psychologist. Not an entrepreneur. Not an investor. Not a computer scientist. Not much of a journalist.

I am – insomuch as our disciplinary training is a proxy for our intellectual and our political interests – fascinated by storytelling, particularly in these sorts of hidden histories and lost histories and secret histories and forgotten histories: my grandfather's involvement at Bletchley Park, for example, and more broadly, the role of computer science in surveillance and war.

What stories do we tell? Whose stories get told? How do these stories reflect and construct our world – worlds of science, politics, culture, and of course, education?

I try in my work to trace and retrace the connections through narratives and counter-narratives, through business and bullshit. My keynote this morning is going to try to string together a number of these stories, from history and from theory and from literature and from science.

See, when I heard that the theme of the conference was "Riding Giants," I confess: I didn't think about waves (even though I live in Southern California, in the heart of its surfer culture). I didn't think about the Isaac Newton saying "standing on the shoulders of giants."

I thought about giants the way, I suppose, a folklorist would. Giants – humanlike monsters of massive size and strength. And as such, I want to talk this morning about giants, about ed-tech's monsters and machines.

I want us to think about Bletchley Park on the road to where we find ourselves today, knowing that there are divergent paths and other stories all along the way.

No doubt, we have witnessed in the last few years an explosion in the ed-tech industry and a growing, a renewed interest in ed-tech. Those here at ALT-C know that ed-tech is not new by any means; but there is this sense from many of its newest proponents (particularly in the States) that ed-tech has no history; there is only the now and the future.

Ed-tech now, particularly that which is intertwined with venture capital, is boosted by a powerful forms of storytelling: a disruptive innovation mythology, entrepreneurs' hagiography, design fiction, fantasy. A fantasy that wants to extend its reach into the material world.

Society has been handed a map, if you will, by the technology industry in which we are shown how these brave ed-tech explorers have and will conquer and carve up virtual and physical space. Fantasy.

We are warned of the dragons in dangerous places, the unexplored places, the over explored places, the stagnant, the lands of outmoded ideas – all the places where we should no longer venture. *Hic Sunt Dracones*. There be dragons.

Instead, I'd argue, we need to face our dragons. We need to face our monsters. We need to face the giants. They aren't simply on the margins; they are, in many ways, central to the map, to the narrative.

I'm in the middle of writing a book called *Teaching Machines*, a cultural history of the science and politics of ed-tech. An anthropology of ed-tech even, a book that looks at knowledge and power and practices, learning and politics and pedagogy. My book explores the push for efficiency and automation in education: intelligent tutoring systems, artificially intelligent textbooks, robot-graders, and robot-readers.

This involves, of course, a nod to "the father of computer science" Alan Turing, who worked at Bletchley Park of course, and his profoundly significant question "Can a machine think?"

I want to ask in turn, "Can a machine teach?"

Then too: What will happen to humans when (if) machines do "think"? What will happen to humans when (if) machines "teach"? What will happen to labor and what happens to learning?

And what exactly do we mean by those verbs "think" and "teach"? When we see signs of thinking or teaching in machines, what does that really signal? Is it that our machines are becoming more "intelligent," more human? Or is it perhaps that humans are becoming more mechanical?

Rather than speculate about the future of thinking and teaching machines, I want to talk a bit about the past.

Long before Bletchley Park or Alan Turing or the Colossus, machines have spoken in binary – ones and zeroes. Quite recently I literally etched this into my skin with two tattoos that "speak" to me while I write.

My left forearm, in binary, a quotation from Walt Whitman's "Leaves of Grass": "Resist much, obey little."

01010010 01100101 01110011 01101001 01110011 01110100 00100000
01101101 01110101 01100011 01101000 00101100 00100000 01101111
01100010 01100101 01111001 00100000 01101100 01101001 01110100
01110100 01101100 01100101

My right forearm, in binary, a quotation from Lord Byron's "Song of the Luddites": "Down with all kings but King Ludd."

01000001 01101110 01100100 00100000 01100100 01101111 01110111
01101110 00100000 01110111 01101001 01110100 01101000 00100000
01100001 01101100 01101100 00100000 01101011 01101001 01101110
01100111 01110011 00100000 01100010 01110101 01110100 00100000
01001011 01101001 01101110 01100111 00100000 01001100 01110101 01110101
01100100 01100100 00100001

Poetry. Bodies. Resistance. Machines.

Lord Byron was one of the very few defenders of the Luddites. His only appearance in the House of Lords was to give a speech challenging the 1812 Frame Breaking Act, which made destruction of mechanized looms punishable by death.

Ah the Luddites, those 19th century artisans who protested against the introduction of factory-owned "labor-saving" textile machines. And the emphasis, let's be clear, should be on "labor" here, less on "machine." The Luddites sought to protect their livelihoods, and they demanded higher wages in the midst of economic upheaval, mass unemployment, and the long Napoleonic Wars. They were opposed to the factories, to the newly-formed corporations owning the means of production, to the mechanized looms.

The Luddites were not really "anti-technology" per se, although that's what the word has come to mean. From the *Oxford English Dictionary*: "Luddite: A member of an organized band of English mechanics and their friends, who (1811–16) set themselves to destroy manufacturing machinery in the midlands and north of England." The etymology: from the proper name Ludd with the suffix -ite.

"According to Pellew's *Life of Lord Sidmouth* (1847) Ned Lud was a person of weak intellect who lived in a Leicestershire village about 1779, and who in a fit of insane rage rushed into a 'stockinger's' house, and destroyed two frames so completely that the saying 'Lud must have been here' came to be used throughout the hosiery districts when a stocking-frame had undergone extraordinary damage. The story lacks confirmation. It appears that in 1811–13 the nickname 'Captain Ludd' or 'King Lud' was commonly given to the ringleaders of the Luddites."

Ludd was, as this image shows, often portrayed as a giant.

Today we use the word "Luddite" in what the OED calls the "transferred sense": One who opposes the introduction of new technology, especially into a place of work.

The sample usage the OED offers, from *The Economist* in 1986: "By suggesting ... that the modern world has lost control of its technology, both [accidents] help to strengthen the hands of Luddites who would halt technology and therefore a lot of economic growth."

To oppose technology or to fear automation, some like *The Economist* or venture capitalist Marc Andreessen argue, is to misunderstand how the economy works. (I would counter that Luddites understand how the economy works quite well, thank you very much, particularly when it comes to questions of "who owns the machinery" we now must work on. Certainly the economy works well for Marc Andreessen.)

In 1984 American novelist Thomas Pynchon asked, "Is it ok to be a Luddite?" suggesting that, in the new Computer Age, it well may be that we have mostly lost our "Luddite sensibility." We no longer resist or rage against the machines. But he adds that we might some day need to. He writes, "If our world survives, the next great challenge to watch out for will come – you heard it here first – when the curves of research and development in artificial intelligence, molecular biology and robotics all converge. Oboy. It will be amazing and unpredictable, and even the biggest of brass, let us devoutly hope, are going to be caught flat-footed. It is certainly something for all good Luddites to look forward to if, God willing, we should live so long."

And here we are, 30 years after Pynchon's essay, facing pronouncements and predictions that our jobs – and not just the factory jobs, but the white collar jobs as well – are soon to be automated. "We are entering a new phase in world history – one in which fewer and fewer workers will be needed to produce the goods and services for the global population," write Erik Brynjolfsson and Andrew McAfee in their book *Race Against the Machine*. "Before the end of this century," says *Wired Magazine*'s Kevin Kelly, "70 percent of today's occupations will ... be replaced by automation." *The Economist* offers a more rapid timeline. "Nearly half of American jobs could be automated in a decade or two," it contends.

We are, some say, on the cusp of a great revolution in artificial intelligence and as such a great revolution in human labor. (Of course, the history of AI is full of predictions that are "two decades" away, but there you go. Like I said earlier, our technological storytelling is fantasy, fantastic.)

So thank you, Alan Turing, for laying the philosophical groundwork for AI. And thank you – ironically – Lord Byron.

Lord Byron was the father of Ada Lovelace. Ada Lovelace worked with Charles Babbage on his Analytical Engine. Ada Lovelace is often credited as the first computer programmer.

As we celebrate – probably the wrong verb – 200 years of Luddism, we should recall too another bicentenary that's approaching. Lord Byron was there for that as well, when a small group of friends – Percy Bysshe Shelley, John William Polidori, Claire Clairmont, Mary Godwin – spent the summer of 1816 in Lake Geneva, Switzerland – "a wet, ungenial summer" – when they all decided to try their hands at writing ghost stories. There, Mary Godwin, later Mary Shelley, wrote *Frankenstein*, published in 1818, arguably the first work of science fiction and certainly one of the most important and influential texts on science, technology, and monsters.

Monsters, mind you, not machines.

"However much of *Frankenstein*'s longevity is owing to the undersung genius James Whale who translated it to film," writes Pynchon in his essay on Luddites, "it remains today more than well worth reading, for all the reasons we read novels, as well as for the much more limited question of its Luddite value: that is, for its attempt, through literary means which are nocturnal and deal in disguise, to deny the machine."

While the laboratory visualized in Whale's 1931 film is full of electrical and mechanical equipment, machines are largely absent from Mary Shelley's novel. There are just a few passing mentions of the equipment necessary to cause that great "Galvanic twitch," a couple of references to lightning, but that's it. Pynchon argues that this absence is purposeful, that this aspect of the Gothic literary genre represented "deep and religious yearnings for that earlier mythic time which had come to be known as the Age of Miracles."

"To insist on the miraculous," argues Pynchon, "is to deny to the machine at least some of its claims on us, to assert the limited wish that living things, earthly and otherwise, may on occasion become Bad and Big enough to take part in transcendent doings."

But even without machines, *Frankenstein* is still read as a cautionary tale about science and about technology; and Shelley's story has left an indelible impression on us. Its references are scattered throughout popular culture and popular discourse. We frequently use part of the title – "Franken" – to invoke a frightening image of scientific experimentation gone wrong. Frankenfood. Frankenfish. The monster, a monstrosity – a technological crime against nature.

It is telling, very telling, that we often confuse the scientist, Victor Frankenstein, with his creation. We often call the monster Frankenstein.

As the sociologist Bruno Latour has argued, we don't merely mistake the identity of Frankenstein; we also mistake his crime. It "was not that he invented a creature through some combination of hubris and high technology," writes Latour, "but rather that he abandoned the creature to itself."

The creature – again, a giant – insists in the novel that he was not born a monster, but he became monstrous after Frankenstein fled the laboratory in horror when the creature opened his "dull yellow eye," breathed hard, and convulsed to life.

"Remember that I am thy creature," he says when he confronts Frankenstein, "I ought to be thy Adam; but I am rather the fallen angel, whom thou drivest from joy for no misdeed. Everywhere I see bliss, from which I alone am irrevocably excluded. I was benevolent and good – misery made me a fiend."

As Latour observes, "Written at the dawn of the great technological revolutions that would define the 19th and 20th centuries, *Frankenstein* foresees that the gigantic sins that were to be committed would hide a much greater sin. It is not the case that we have failed to care for Creation, but that we have failed to care for our technological creations. We confuse the monster for its creator and blame our sins against Nature upon our creations. But our sin is not that we created technologies but that we failed to love and care for them. It is as if we decided that we were unable to follow through with the education of our children."

Our "gigantic sin": we failed to love and care for our technological creations. We must love and educate our children. We must love and care for our machines, lest they become monsters.

Indeed, *Frankenstein* is also a novel about education. The novel is structured as a series of narratives – Captain Watson's story – a letter he sends to his sister as he explores the Arctic – which then tells Victor Frankenstein's story through which we hear the creature tell his own story, along with that of the De Lacey family and the arrival of Safie, "the lovely Arabian." All of these are stories about education: some self-directed learning, some through formal schooling.

While typically *Frankenstein* is interpreted as a condemnation of science gone awry, the novel can also be read as a condemnation of education gone awry. The novel highlights the dangerous consequences of scientific knowledge, sure, but it also explores how knowledge – gained inadvertently, perhaps, gained surreptitiously, gained without guidance – might be disastrous. Victor Frankenstein, stumbling across the alchemists and then having their work dismissed outright by his father, stoking his curiosity. The creature, learning to speak by watching the De Lacey family, learning to read by watching Safie do the same, his finding and reading Volney's *Ruins of Empires* and Milton's *Paradise Lost*.

"Oh, that I had forever remained in my native wood, nor known or felt beyond the sensations of hunger, thirst, and heat!" the creature cries.

In his article "Love Your Monsters," Latour argues that *Frankenstein* is a "parable for political ecology." Again, the lesson of the novel is not that we should step away from technological innovation or scientific creation. But rather we must strengthen our commitment and our patience and our commitment to all of creation – capital C creation – now includes, Latour suggests, our technological creations, our machines.

Is *Frankenstein* a similarly useful parable for education technology? What are we to make of ed-tech's monsters, of our machines? Is there something to be said here about pedagogy, technologies, and an absence of care?

200 years of Luddites, 200 years of *Frankenstein* and – by my calculations at least – 150 some-odd years of "teaching machines."

To be clear, my nod to the Luddites or to *Frankenstein* isn't about rejecting technology; but it is about rejecting exploitation. It is about rejecting an uncritical and unexamined belief in progress. The problem isn't that science gives us monsters, it's that we have pretended like it is truth and divorced from responsibility, from love, from politics, from care. The problem isn't that science gives us monsters, it's that it does not, despite its insistence, give us "the answer."

And that is problem with ed-tech's monsters. That is the problem with teaching machines.

In order to automate education, must we see knowledge in a certain way, as certain: atomistic, programmable, deliverable, hierarchical, fixed, measurable, non-negotiable? In order to automate that knowledge, what happens to care?

Although teaching machines predate his work by almost a century, they are most often associated with the behaviorist Harvard psychology professor B. F. Skinner.

An excerpt from Ayn Rand's review of B. F. Skinner's 1971 book *Beyond Freedom and Dignity*: "The book itself is like Boris Karloff's embodiment of Frankenstein's monster," Rand writes, "a corpse patched with nuts, bolts and screws from the junkyard of philosophy (Pragmatism, Social Darwinism, Positivism, Linguistic Analysis, with some nails by Hume, threads by Russell, and glue by the *New York Post*). The book's voice, like Karloff's, is an emission of inarticulate, moaning growls – directed at a special enemy: 'Autonomous Man.'"

I quote Rand's stinging criticism of Skinner because of the Frankenstein reference, clearly: the accusation of a misbegotten creation of a misbegotten science. B. F. Skinner as Frankenstein. Rand implies here, with a fairly typical invocation of the film, that Skinner's work is an attempt to "play God." And we might see, as Rand suggests, Skinner's creations as monsters – with a fixation on control, a rejection of freedom, and an absence of emotion or care.

To be clear, I quote Ayn Rand here with a great deal of irony. The Silicon Valley technology industry these days seems full of those touting her objectivist, laissez-faire version of libertarianism, her radical individualism. (Monstrous in its own right.)

Rand uses Skinner as an example of the ills of federally-funded research. She insists she does not want to "censor research projects" but instead to "abolish all government subsidies in the field of the social sciences." A "free marketplace of ideas" where things like behaviorism will lose.

But the "free marketplace of ideas" that a lot of libertarian tech types now want too actually values behaviorism quite a bit.

Rand criticizes Skinner for arguing that there is no freedom, that we are always controlled, that we should hand over our lives to scientific management full of "positive reinforcers." For this behaviorist control, Rand will not stand.

But behaviorist control mechanisms run throughout our technologies: gamification, notifications, nudges.

The Turing Test – that foundational test in artificial intelligence – is, one might argue, a behaviorist test. The question isn't, Alan Turing argued, "can a machine think?" but rather "can a machine exhibit intelligent *behaviors* and fool a human into thinking the machine is human?" [Emphasis mine]

Again, monsters and machines.

Before developing teaching machines, Skinner had worked on a number of projects, inventing as part of his graduate work, what's now known as "the Skinner Box" around 1930. "The operant conditioning chamber," the Skinner Box was used to study and to train animals to perform certain tasks. Do it correctly; get a reward (namely food).

During World War II, Skinner worked on Project Pigeon, an experimental project to create pigeon-guided missiles.

I cannot begin to tell you how much I wish I could have talked with my grandfather about Bletchley Park. Even more, how much I wish I could have asked him his thoughts about pigeons and radar.

The military canceled and revived Project Pigeon a couple of times. "Our problem," said Skinner, "was no one would take us seriously." Go figure. By 1953, the military had devised an electronic system for missile guidance, and animal-guided systems were no longer necessary.

That same year, Skinner came up with the idea for his teaching machine. Visiting his daughter's fourth grade classroom, he was struck by the inefficiencies. Not only were all the students expected to move through their lessons at the same pace, but when it came to assignments and quizzes, they did not receive feedback until the teacher had graded the materials – sometimes a delay of days. Skinner believed that both of these flaws in school could be addressed through a machine, and built a prototype that he demonstrated at a conference the following year.

All these elements were part of Skinner's teaching machines: the elimination of inefficiencies of the teacher, the delivery of immediate feedback, the ability for students to move through standardized content at their own pace.

Today's ed-tech proponents call this "personalization."

Addressing social problems, including problems like school, for Skinner meant addressing behaviors. As he wrote in *Beyond Freedom and Dignity*, "We need to make vast changes in human behavior. . . . What we need is a technology of behavior." Teaching machines are one such technology.

Teaching, with or without machines, was viewed by Skinner as reliant on a "contingency of reinforcement." The problems with human teachers' reinforcement, he argued, were severalfold. First, the reinforcement did not occur immediately; that is, as Skinner observed in his daughter's classroom, there was a delay between students completing assignments and quizzes and their work being corrected and returned. Second, much of the focus on behavior in the classroom has to do with punishing students for "bad behavior" rather than rewarding them for good.

"Any one who visits the lower trades of the average school today will observe that a change has been made, not from aversive to positive control, but from one form of aversive stimulation to another," Skinner writes. But with the application of behaviorism and the development of teaching machines, "There is no reason," he insisted, "why the schoolroom should be any less mechanized than, for example, the kitchen."

But maybe there *are* reasons.

Maybe monsters and Luddites can help us formulate our response to Skinner.

According to Google Ngrams, a tool that tracks the frequency of words in the corpus of books that the company has digitized, as society became more industrialized, we steadily and increasingly talked about Luddites, a reflection dare I say, of longstanding concerns about the changing nature of work and society. Increasing, that is, until the turn of the 21st century, when according to Google at least and to paraphrase Dr. Strangelove, we learned to stop worrying and love the machine.

By "love" here, I mean fascination. An enchantment with the shiny and the new. Acquiescence, not engagement, be it political, scientific, or sociological.

This is not what Bruno Latour meant when he told us to "love our monsters."

As our interest in Luddites seemingly declines, I fear, we face what Frankenstein counseled against: a refusal to take responsibility. We see technology as an autonomous creation, one that will move society (and school) forward under its own steam and without our guidance.

Wired Magazine's Kevin Kelly offers perhaps the clearest example of this in his book *What Technology Wants*. Technology, he writes, "has its own wants. It wants to sort itself out, to self-assemble into hierarchical levels, just as most large, deeply interconnected systems do. The technium also wants what every living system wants: to perpetuate itself, to keep itself going. And as it grows, those inherent wants are gaining in complexity and force."

That, I think, is monstrous. That is Frankenstein's monster.

Kelley later tells us, "We can choose to modify our legal and political and economic assumptions to meet the ordained trajectories [of technology] ahead. But we cannot escape from them."

Throw up our hands and surrender, this argument suggests. Surrender to "progress," to the machine.

But it is a slight-of-hand to maintain that technological changes are "what technology wants." It's an argument that obscures what industry, business, systems, power want. It is intellectually disingenuous. It is politically dangerous.

What does a "teaching machine" want, for example? Or to change the sentence slightly, "what does a 'teaching machine' demand?"

I'll echo Catherine Cronin who yesterday said that education demands our political interest and engagement. I insist too that technology demands our political interest and engagement. And to echo Latour again, "our sin is not that we created technologies but that we failed to love and care for them. It is as if we decided that we were unable to follow through with the education of our children." Political interest and engagement is love; it is love for the world. Love, and perhaps some Luddism.

I'll leave you with one final quotation, from Hannah Arendt who wrote, "Education is the point at which we decide whether we love the world enough to assume responsibility for it and by the same token save it from that ruin which, except for renewal, except for the coming of the new and young, would be inevitable. And education, too, is where we decide whether we love our children enough not to expel them from our world and leave them to their own devices, nor to strike from their hands their chance of undertaking something new, something unforeseen by us, but to prepare them in advance for the task of renewing a common world."

Our task, I believe, is to tell the stories and build the society that would place education technology in that same light. "renewing a common world."

We in ed-tech must face the monsters we have created, I think. These are the monsters in the technologies of war and surveillance à la Bletchley Park. These are the monsters in the technologies of mass production and standardization. These are the monsters in the technologies of behavior modification à la BF Skinner.

These are the monsters ed-tech must face. And we must all consider what we need to do so that we do not create more of them.

This keynote was delivered on September 3, 2014 at the ALT Conference in Coventry, UK. The original transcript, along with the slides, can be found on Hack Education at http://hackeducation.com/2014/09/03/monsters-altc2014/

WORKS CITED

Hannah Arendt, "The Crisis in Education," 1954.

Erik Brynjolfsson and Andrew McAfee, *Race Against the Machine: How the Digital Revolution is Accelerating Innovation, Driving Productivity, and Irreversibly Transforming Employment and the Economy.* Digital Frontier Press. 2011.

Kevin Kelly, "Better Than Human: Why Robots Will – And Must – Take Our Jobs." *Wired.* December 2012. http://www.wired.com/2012/12/ff-robots-will-take-our-jobs/all/

Kevin Kelly, *What Technology Wants.* Penguin Books, 2011.

Bruno Latour, "Love Your Monsters," The Breakthrough Institute. Winter 2012. http://thebreakthrough.org/index.php/journal/past-issues/issue-2/love-your-monsters

Thomas Pynchon, "Is It OK to Be a Luddite?" *The New York Times.* October 28, 1984. http://www.nytimes.com/books/97/05/18/reviews/pynchon-luddite.html

Ayn Rand, "The Stimulus and the Response: A Critique of B.F. Skinner," *Philosophy: Who Needs It.* http://www.sntp.net/behaviorism/ayn_rand_skinner.htm

Mary Shelley, *Frankenstein.* Dover Thrift Editions, 1994 (1818).

B. F. Skinner, *Beyond Freedom and Dignity.* Hackett Publishing Company, 1971.

Alan Turing, "Computing machinery and intelligence." *Mind,* 1950. Vol. 59, 433-460.

10 THE FUTURE OF EDUCATION: PROGRAMMED OR PROGRAMMABLE

When people ask me how I ended up becoming an education technology writer, I'm never quite sure how to answer. I don't have a degree in "education" or "technology" or even "writing." I sometimes joke that I took an aptitude test in junior high that gave me one career option – freelance writer – result that, truth be told, caused me at the time to panic a bit and dismiss the idea altogether.

So there wasn't really one moment when I decided this was what I was going to do, and there isn't really a clear path that I can trace for you that got me to where I am today. Instead, there were lots of little episodes, things I didn't always think deeply about at the time, that have shaped my views about education and technology and that have prompted me to ask, "Wait, what are we doing? Why?" and then to write about it online.

So let me tell you a story about one of those little episodes – a story that I hope can be useful at cracking open those questions "What are we doing" in ed-tech and "Why":

In 1991 after two years of university back east, I dropped out of school. About a year later, I had a baby. I moved back to Wyoming, where I was born and where my folks lived. I recognized that I would need to get a college degree, particularly if I ever wanted to "escape" my hometown again. But Wyoming only has one university, and it was 150 miles away from where I lived. I didn't want to relocate, I couldn't really relocate, so instead I enrolled at the local community college that had just launched an outreach program in association with UW, offering a handful of bachelor's degrees.

The outreach program was geared towards what we sometimes call "non-traditional" or "adult" learners, so many of the classes were held in the evenings or on weekends. And as the community college hadn't really built out a large faculty for teaching upper division classes, a number of our courses were offered via "distance education," with an instructor and classes in community college campuses across the state connected through the wonderful, cutting-edge technology of the conference call. We were also encouraged to take advantage of correspondence courses from other regional universities.

I'd heard some not-too-nice things about the community college statistics instructor, so I decided to take Introduction to Statistics through a correspondence course. I received in the mail a giant box containing the textbook, the worksheets I needed to complete and return to the professor, and half a dozen or so videotapes containing all his lectures.

I really had a hard time with the course.

I know this experience colors my views on online education today, particularly when I hear that some combination of videos and exercises – whether it be Khan Academy or MOOCs – is going to make us all more adept at math and science and engineering. I just don't believe that the ability to rewind or replay a video is that useful in helping a student struggling to understand a concept. Me, I rewound and replayed those statistics videos a lot. It didn't help.

But my experience with the correspondence course did help me understand, I think for the first time in my life as a student, how our models and our theories and our practices in education shape and are shaped by the technologies we use.

Receiving this box of materials in the mail was a literalization of the idea that education involves "content delivery." That is, the courseware for Intro to Statistics was quite literally delivered to my doorstep. I'd insert the videotapes into the VCR, and the content would be delivered to my living room and purportedly into my brain. "Content delivery" is not always quite so literally enacted, of course, but it's still the paradigm education largely operates within.

This is not a new paradigm, of course. But for me this was the moment – looking with frustration at this this box of videotapes – in which I realized that that's what education privileges.

Whether it's in a textbook or in a video-taped lecture, it's long been the content that matters most in school. The content is central. It's what you go to school to be exposed to. Content. The student must study it, comprehend it, and demonstrate that in turn for the teacher. That is what we expect an education to do, to be: the acquisition of content that becomes transmogrified into knowledge. (The focus is certain content, of course and thus certain knowledge – that which has been decreed significant by a host of institutional, cultural, historical, political, intellectual forces.)

That model of thinking about teaching and learning and arranging courses and classrooms is incredibly old. And despite all of the hype and hoopla about new technologies disrupting old models of education, we see this fixation on knowledge acquisition becoming hard-coded into our practices in the latest ed-tech software – software that now promises to make the process more "personalized" and more efficient.

That is, despite all the potential to do things differently with computers and with the Internet and with ubiquitous digital information, school still puts content in the center. Content, once delivered by or mediated through a teacher or a textbook, now is delivered via various computer technologies.

One more story from my time at Casper College: In 1994, Congress passed the Violent Crime Control and Law Enforcement Act, the largest crime bill in the history of the US. It's best known for its ban on assault weapons. But one "small" provision ended the ability for prison inmates to receive Pell Grants.

Prior to that, inmates did often pursue their degrees through distance education classes. I know, because thanks to distance education, I had classes with them.

I still remember the first evening of my Political Violence course, as the professor asked all the students in the various remote campus locations to identify themselves. A couple from Riverton. A couple from Sheridan. One from Powell. And there were three students on the conference call from the Wyoming State Penitentiary. Three inmates. Three students. Let me tell you: our class discussions of terrorism, gun ownership, police violence, political activism, war, the legal system, and the death penalty were much, much richer for their presence.

That's an important shift in the model of education. The content – the assigned readings, the lectures, the videos – were not, could not possibly be the center of that class. The content could not be "delivered," because our analysis of political violence had to be constructed and deconstructed and negotiated, with full recognition of those who were in the class and had experienced, enacted forms of political violence – whether those students were in the pen or not.

The class, connected through telephony, was networked, as in turn was the learning.

Peer learning, networked learning. We talk a lot about these quite a bit in ed-tech today. We make some gestures to that end – the possibilities afforded to us, not so much by conference calls, but by newer forms of connectivity. By the Internet.

But more often than not, we still lasso technology for the more traditional purposes and practices of education: for content delivery. We keep designing education technology with an emphasis on knowledge acquisition, despite all our glee about a move into an information age where our relationship to knowledge will supposedly be transformed.

We are still designing ed-tech for the past and not for the present and certainly not for the future.

EDUCATION THEORIES / ED-TECH MODELS

So these are the two models of ed-tech I want to talk about tonight: programmed instruction and the programmable web.

I realize, of course, that I'm making an all-too-tidy divide, as though there are just two theories, two models, two visions, two technologies, two choices, two futures.

And yes I'm using these phrases as shorthand, recognizing that they both have their own complex meanings and histories and pedagogies and ideologies and practices. But I firmly believe that these are histories and pedagogies and ideologies and practices that we in ed-tech need to pay much more attention to.

ED-TECH AS PROGRAMMED INSTRUCTION

Most education technology today, particularly that which is used in classrooms, would fall into the "programmed instruction" category. And frankly that shouldn't surprise us. If you buy my premise that education has been and is focused on "content delivery" – you needn't, of course – then an embrace of programmed instruction certainly makes sense.

Programmed instruction is a technological intervention in that content delivery mechanism.

As my experience with the Intro to Statistics videos underscores, programmed instruction pre-dates the Web. It pre-dates the computer. It is, I contend, the driving force behind the development of the field of education technology throughout most of the twentieth century.

Education psychologist Edward Thorndike wrote in 1912 that "If, by a miracle of mechanical ingenuity, a book could be so arranged that only to him who had done what was directed on page one would page two become visible, and so on, much that now requires personal instruction could be managed by print."

And a decade later, Thomas Edison said "I believe that the motion picture is destined to revolutionize our educational system and that in a few years it will supplant largely, if not entirely, the use of textbooks. I should say that on the average we get about two percent efficiency out of schoolbooks as they are written today. The education of the future, as I see it, will be conducted through the medium of the motion picture ... where it should be possible to obtain one hundred percent efficiency."

Here we can see the origins – the original aspirations, even – of ed-tech:

the idea that some sort of mechanism could be developed to not only deliver content – that's what Edison imagines – but to handle both instruction and assessment. As such, Thorndike's comment anticipates the development of the teaching machines of the 1920s and thereafter. You can draw a straight line, in fact, between Thorndike and behaviorist B. F. Skinner, the name mostly commonly associated with "teaching machines" and the person who coined the phrase "programmed instruction."

Skinner devised the idea for the teaching machine after visiting his young daughter's classroom and observing what he thought were the "inefficiencies" in it. Students all had to move at the same pace, he said, and when they completed assignments and quizzes, they did not receive immediate feedback and instead had to wait until the teacher had graded and returned the work – days later – to see how well they'd done.

Skinner's machine offered educational materials broken down into the smallest possible steps. To move through the materials, students had to correctly answer the questions presented by the machine. A correct answer would reveal the next question, and the student could move on.

This, of course, fits with Skinner's theories of behaviorism and his notions of operant conditioning. All teaching, with or without mechanical intervention, was viewed by Skinner as reliant on a "contingency of reinforcement." The problems with human teachers' reinforcement, Skinner argued, were severalfold. First, the reinforcement did not occur immediately; that is, as Skinner had observed in his daughter's classroom, there was a delay between students completing assignments and quizzes and their work being corrected and returned. Second, much of the focus on behavior (as it is traditionally defined) in the classroom has to do with punishing students for bad behavior rather than rewarding them for good.

"Any one who visits the lower trades of the average school today will observe that a change has been made, not from aversive to positive control, but from one form of aversive stimulation to another," Skinner wrote. Operant conditioning could train students to work better, just as Skinner had trained pigeons. And with the application of behaviorism and the development of teaching machines, "There is no reason," he insisted, "why the schoolroom should be any less mechanized than, for example, the kitchen."

The development of teaching machines and programmed instruction would lead to a new profession, something that Simon Ramo called in a 1957 essay a "teaching engineer" – "that kind of engineering which is concerned with the educational process and with the design of the machines, as well as the design of the material."

(A bit of trivia for you: Simon Ramo received a patent for one of his ed-tech inventions at age 100. He is also often called "the father of the intercontinental ballistic missile." The connection between the military and ed-tech is a story for another day, another book.)

So there we have it: the birth of the instructional technologist. Note the focus in that phrase on instruction and technology (not on, say, learning and technology.) Designing the machine. Designing the material. Despite the intervening decades, instructional technology is not so far removed from programmed instruction, and the profession needs to wrestle with that, I think.

ED-TECH AND THE PROGRAMMABLE WEB

Programmed instruction reflects and reinforces – as I suggested earlier, hard-codes even – content as the center of learning, the center of certain theories of learning and of their associated classroom practices. Content is at the heart of many of the mechanisms we've spent the last hundred years or so building to aid education. Content continues to be at the heart of many new mechanisms as well.

But I think new technologies and – let's give recognition where recognition is due – many older learning theories have demonstrated that there are alternatives.

Think back to my anecdote about the class discussions with my peers in the penitentiary. The network there was enabled by conference calls. Today, we're more likely to point to the Internet, not the telephone, as the technology that enables networked communication.

But I want to specifically talk about the Web, which is – or could be, at least – a significant shift away from programmed instruction.

And the shift isn't simply about a new technology for content delivery. It isn't about giving Classroom A access to Digital Content B or connecting Classroom A with Classroom B so they can jointly listen to the same lecture. Despite the ease of distribution that comes with Internet technologies, these examples still position content in the center of the educational enterprise. We can't act as though "access" to content is the pinnacle of what new technologies can afford us. We can't act as though "digital distribution" of content is the pinnacle either.

I want to posit as an oppositional force, a resistance, an alternative to "programmed instruction" – all that history of Skinner and textbooks and testing: the "programmable web."

What's interesting and important and (in my most hopeful moments I can even say) potentially transformative about the Web isn't just that we are networked. It's that the pages that we can load in our browsers can be read and can be written. They can be written in human language; and they can be scripted in computer language.

The phrase "Web 2.0," coined circa 1999 – the read/write Web – feels more than a little passé in 2014, particularly as we see the corporate vultures who've swooped in to redefine what "social" looks like online and to encourage us to read and write in their information silos.

But the readable, writable, programmable Web is an important development in education technology. Perhaps one of the most important. As such, we can't just let that go. We can't just surrender the Web to the technology industry or the advertising industry, just as we shouldn't surrender ed-tech to programmed instruction.

The readable, writable, programmable Web is so significant because, in part, it allows us to break from programmed instruction. That is, we needn't all simply be on the receiving end of some computer-mediated instruction, some teacher-engineering. We can construct and create and connect for ourselves. And that means that ideally we can move beyond the technologies that deliver content more efficiently, more widely. It means too we can rethink "content" and "information" and "knowledge" – what it means to deliver or consume those things, alongside what it makes to build and control those things.

One of the most powerful things that you can do on the Web is to be a node in a network of learners, and to do so most fully and radically, I dare say, you must own your own domain.

I think we've been taught that owning a domain is beyond the reach of most of us – we don't have the technical skills to manage servers, DNS, databases, and the like. Again, we're told we should leave it to the engineers. But there are a growing number of tools and services that make owning and managing your own domain quite doable.

Supporting students in owning their own domain is one of the most important things we in education technology can do. We can frame this, at the very least, as giving them "skills" that will be useful in their personal and professional lives, but the implications are much broader.

I typically point to the University of Mary Washington as an example of a school that gets this and that is leading the way for others. UWM gives each faculty and student their own domain – and I don't mean simply a space on the university's servers under the university's domain. UWM helps everyone buy the domain of their choosing, and they host it for the duration that the student is enrolled. They offer a simple interface that helps with installing open source software like WordPress. And then when a student graduates, everything – all the content that a student has created, everything they've uploaded onto their site – can go with them, as UWM hands them the keys to their domain. It is theirs.

Thanks to technologies like RSS – short for Rich Site Summary or Really Simple Syndication – one can weave together the output from these spaces, syndicating them into one place. While the content remains distributed, housed on individual blogs, feeds can pull copies into a centralized site. This is how the University of Mary Washington manages blog posts for many of its courses. Students blog on their own sites but tag their posts with keywords associated with a particular course. An RSS feed then pulls content with that keyword into a course website. That's a different model – technologically and pedagogically as well.

Learning on the Web means that the intellectual relationship isn't restricted to student and content. The relationship isn't only among student, content, and instructor. The exchange isn't about a student demonstrating to an instructor that content has been "successfully delivered" and processed. Learning on the Web opens that intellectual exchange up in new ways. Authority, expertise, participation, voice – these can be so different on the programmable web; not so with programmed instruction.

The Domain of One's Own initiative at University of Mary Washington purposefully invokes Virginia Woolf's *A Room of One's Own*: "A woman must have money, and a room of her own, if she is to write fiction." That is, one needs a space – a safe space that one controls – in order to do be intellectually productive.

Intellectual productivity on the Web looks a bit different, no doubt, but there is this notion, embedded in the Domain of One's Own project, that it is important to have one's own space in order to develop one's ideas and one's craft. It's important that, as learners, we have control over our content and our data. We aren't simply receptacles for content delivery mechanisms, as imaged by the machines of programmed instruction; and we aren't simply the sources for learning outcomes and learning analytics – data that can be used to feed the new algorithms of today's fancier teaching machines.

Having one's own domain means too that we have much more say over what we present to the world – in terms of our "public profile," our professional portfolio, what have you. Control over the look and feel of the site. Control over the content. Control over what's shared. Control – a bit more control, not total – over one's data.

If we are to resist "programmed instruction" – or at least do things differently in this so-called information age – we shouldn't just talk about new education technologies that do the same old thing, but more efficiently. We have an amazing opportunity here. We need to recognize and reconcile that, for starters, in the content that programmed instruction – as with all instruction – delivers, there is a hidden curriculum nestled in there as well. Education – formal institutions of schooling – is very much about power, prestige, and control.

If we see learning as a process that develops the self, then control over that process and then control over the presentation of that self seems crucial. Again, this is why owning one's own domain on the Web is so important.

And it's something that we need to scrutinize in education technology –

in all technology, really. Programmed instruction doesn't simply fix the content; it fixes the relationship between learner and instructor (whether machine or human). There is no reciprocity there, for starters. And there's little opportunity to express oneself outside the pre-ordained, the pre-programmed design.

Ed-tech works like this: you sign up for a service and you're flagged as either "teacher" or "student" or "admin." Depending on that role, you have different "privileges" – that's an important word, because it doesn't simply imply what you can and cannot do with the software. It's a nod to political power, social power as well.

Many pieces of software, despite their invocation of "personalization," present you with a very restricted, restrictive set of choices of who you "can be." It's what cyborg anthropologist Amber Case calls the "templated self." She explains this as"

"A self or identity that is produced through various participation architectures, the act of producing a virtual or digital representation of self by filling out a user interface with personal information.

Facebook and Twitter are examples of the templated self. The shape of a space affects how one can move, what one does and how one interacts with someone else. It also defines how influential and what constraints there are to that identity. A more flexible, but still templated space is WordPress. A hand-built site is much less templated, as one is free to fully create their digital self in any way possible. Those in Second Life play with and modify templated selves into increasingly unique online identities. MySpace pages are templates, but the lack of constraints can lead to spaces that are considered irritating to others."

While Case's examples here point to mostly "social" technologies, education technologies also serve as "participation architectures." How do these technologies produce a digital representation of the learner-self?

Of course, you could argue that the education system is already incredibly interested in "templating" students as well as "templating" knowledge. We see this in graduation requirements, course requirements, essay requirements, disciplinary requirements, tenure requirements, and so on. Many education technologies loyally re-inscribe these into the digital world. The LMS is perhaps the perfect example. The call for more adaptive technologies (often connected to textbook, assessment, and LMS technologies), reliant as they are on data models and algorithms, are the next wave of tools that produce the "templated learner."

Programmed instruction has long sought to work to that end, but this architecture now extends elsewhere.

Programmed instruction programs the learner. Necessarily. By design.

The programmable web need not.

I don't want to overreach here and make an argument that the Web is

105

some sort of technological or ed-tech utopia. Despite all the talk about "leveling the playing field" and disrupting old, powerful institutions, the Web replicates many pre-existing inequalities; it exacerbates others; it creates new ones. I think we have to work much harder to make the Web live up to the rhetoric of freedom and equality. That's a political effort, not simply a technological one.

Let me repeat that, because it has pretty significant implications for ed-tech, which is so often developed and implemented at the whims of political decisions – decisions made by politicians, administrators, decisions influenced by budgets, vendor pitches, and the latest Thomas Friedman *New York Times* op-ed. Decisions like ending Pell Grants for prisoners, for example.

To transform education and education technology to more progressive and less programmed ends means we do have to address what exactly we think education should look like now and in the future. Do we want programmed instruction? Do we want teaching machines? Do we want videotaped lectures? Do we want content delivery systems? Or do we want education that is more student-centered, more networked-focused. Are we ready to move beyond "content" and even beyond "competencies"? Can we address the ed-tech practices that look more and more like carceral education – surveillance, predictive policing, control?

These are political questions, and they are philosophical questions. I don't think it's quite as simple as a choice between programmed instruction or the programmable web. And instead of acting as though ed-tech is free of ideology, we need to recognize that it is very much enmeshed in it.

This talk was given at Pepperdine University on November 4, 2014. The original transcript can be found on Hack Education at http://www.hackeducation.com/2014/11/04/programmed-instruction-versus-the-programmable-web/

WORKS CITED

Amber Case, "Templated Self," A Dictionary of Cyborg Anthropology. http://cyborganthropology.com/Templated_Self

Larry Cuban, *Teachers and Machines: The Classroom Use of Technology Since 1920.* Teachers College Press, 1986.

A. A. Lumsdaine and Robert Glaser, eds. *Teaching Machines and Programmed Instruction: A Source Book.* Department of Audio-Visual Instruction National

Education Association, 1960.

Paul Saettler, *A History of Instructional Technology*. McGraw-Hill. 1968.

B. F. Skinner, *The Technology of Teaching*. Copley Publishing Group. 1968.

Virginia Woolf, *A Room of One's Own*. 1929.

11 BEYOND THE LMS

I gave a keynote on Wednesday at ALT about "Ed-Tech's Monsters" in which I was reminded by the audience that some of the stories I tell about ed-tech tend to be very American stories. (In my defense, I did cite Roald Dahl and Lord Byron and Mary Shelley and Bruno Latour.) But duly noted. And quite true. I find myself following far too closely for my own mental health the stories out of Silicon Valley.

So as I looked through my notes last night about what I'd planned to talk about today, I realized that I'd probably done it again: I'd prepared a talk that was really about my experiences with American higher education and my experiences with American ed-tech.

I want to say to you here at the outset of my talk how I responded to a question at ALT: I worry that other countries are importing American education policies in the name of austerity and efficiency. I worry that the US, particularly Silicon Valley, is exporting its stories alongside its technologies to the rest of the world as well. It isn't quite cultural imperialism, although I do think that's a part of it that we shouldn't ignore. Computing programming, despite the gesture to "programming languages," is done almost entirely in English after all. I think we're witnessing here a new sort of imperialism – at the level of technology, at the level of infrastructure.

Education has, of course, always been a part of the imperial endeavor. And now, I think, we should talk about how ed-tech might be the newest form of that. Form. Content. Infrastructure. Ideology.

That's not what I planned to talk about today. But it's an important subtext. I'm quite interested in how and if MOOCs built by and built in the UK, for example, can be a strange sort of resistance to this imperialism, or if they are too deeply intertwined in it already.

What I'd like to talk about specifically is how we can move beyond the

108

MOOC, beyond the VLE, beyond the LMS.

The Learning Management System. The LMS. Or in the UK, the VLE. The Virtual Learning Environment.

Even though the latter sounds much less foreboding and less controlling than the former, I confess: it makes little difference to me. I am not a fan.

As a technology writer and observer of the (fairly) thriving education technology startup "scene," one of the things I find both fascinating and frustrating is the number of young education technology entrepreneurs who decide to work in ed-tech because they were, as college students frustrated with the LMS.

Again and again and again, I hear "Blackboard sucks." It's like the one punch-line a comedian can work into any routine: you say something critical about Blackboard and everyone cheers and laughs until they cry.

And I do not disagree. "Blackboard sucks."

The solution then, for many of these entrepreneurs, is to build the same thing, just with a nicer, more modern user interface. "It's like Blackboard," I hear them say, but with the blue colors we now associate with Facebook. "It's like Blackboard" but with a news feed. "It's like Blackboard" but with responsive design or with a mobile app. "It's like Blackboard" but you don't have to have permission from your IT department. "It's like Blackboard" but it's free. But at the end of the day, it's like Blackboard. And that's not particularly interesting or progressive to me.

Blackboard, you'll often here these entrepreneurs say, is "ripe for disruption." The LMS market is huge: several billion dollars a year are spent on these systems. Once sold just to universities, the LMS is now used in corporate learning, and it's increasingly a tool in elementary and secondary education; these companies see a huge potential market in the developing world as well.

With such rampant dissatisfaction with the market leader – with so much bile over Blackboard – it's not that surprising that investors and entrepreneurs alike are keen to try to get a piece of that pie.

I can think of no other company in education – not even Pearson – that elicits as much hatred as Blackboard. And it's hatred that comes from all sorts of users: from students, from teachers, from administrators.

Rather than looking for or building towards a better Blackboard, or a better VLE, I want us to ask why we use these technologies in the first place. And from there, why we'd continue to do so.

These are important questions for us to consider about all technologies. I think we have convinced ourselves that new technologies mean new practices, new affordances. But that's not always or necessarily how technology works. The history of technology suggests otherwise. We often find ourselves adopting new tools that simply perform old tasks a wee bit better, a wee bit faster. Updating your iPhone to the latest model is easy.

Shedding 150 years of cultural practices around telephony, for example, is a lot more challenging. But it happens. Cultural practices do change. I use the phone function quite rarely on my iPhone. In fact, I bristle when it rings.

Technology doesn't simply enable new practices; it shapes, limits, steers our practices, and then – and this is key – even when the technology changes, those practices often endure. Now with computers these practices become "hard coded." They become part of the infrastructure.

The VLE is a wonderfully terrible example of that.

The learning management system has shaped a generation's view of education technology, and I'd contend, shaped it for the worst. It has shaped what many people think ed-tech looks like, how it works, whose needs it suits, what it can do, and why it would do so. The learning management system reflects the technological desires of administrators – it's right there in the phrase. "Management." It does not reflect the needs of teachers and learners.

I admit, I am biased.

I started teaching, as a graduate student at the University of Oregon, in 1999. At the time, the university gave all students and faculty a Web space: www dot uoregon dot edu backspace tilde your username. I was new to the Web (we all were, I suppose). I learned a little HTML from a friend so that I could post my syllabi, handouts, and notes online.

I thought at the time – quite naively – that students would appreciate online accessibility to these materials. There would be no more "Can I get another copy of the syllabus. I lost mine." But I found the students still asked me for printed copies of the materials, even though I assured them that it was all on the Web.

I posted my stuff to the Web too because, as someone new to teaching, I recognized that I relied a lot on my peers to help me think through what exactly I wanted my course to do. (At the time, I was teaching Introduction to College Composition.) I learned a lot by working with more experienced graduate students and instructors, looking at how they organized their courses, how they structured readings, assignments, and assessments. It seemed worthwhile to post all of this on the Web so that anyone – not just my peers in the writing department – could benefit.

But that same year I started teaching – 1999 – the University of Oregon adopted Blackboard. And quickly we heard instruction from above that we were to post all our course materials in Blackboard. Syllabi. Handouts. Readings. Quizzes. Discussion forums. All was to take place behind the wall of the LMS. I don't recall how much of this was a mandate and how much of this was "encouragement" – these are distinctions that graduate students, whose livelihoods and tuition remissions, are probably unlikely to make. If your advisor says do it, you do it. You follow orders. That's how academic hierarchy works.

The Blackboard migration stuck with me: a distaste about whom exactly the LMS was meant to serve.

After all, at the end of each semester, students would lose access to the materials – could lose, I suppose. There are some administrative controls to extend their access. But once a course was closed, anything students had written in the forums, for example, any interactions they had had through the messaging system: gone. And when I left the university, I lost access to all the materials that I'd posted there too. My syllabi, my handouts, the rosters of my students. Gone.

We call those administrative controls "privileges." I think that speaks volumes. Who has privilege, who has power in the design and in the usage of our education technologies?

Some history:

Blackboard was founded in 1997 by Michael Chasen and Matthew Pittinsky, both of whom are still involved in education technology today. At the time, they were consultants for the IMS Global Learning Consortium. In 1998, Blackboard merged with CourseInfo, a course management system spun out of Cornell University that was founded by Daniel Cane and Stephen Gilfus. Gilfus remains an education technology consultant. Cane has now moved on to "modernizing medicine."

The new company Blackboard made a profit its first year. That is pretty noteworthy. I don't think there are too many ed-tech startups that can boast that today.

While there are many examples of course management tools that predate Blackboard and there are examples of Internet-connected learning environments that predate Blackboard, the company was quickly able to gain press like this, from *The Washington Post* in 1999: "Blackboard Chalks Up a Breakthrough; Its Educational Software Lets Colleges Put Classes on the Internet."

Why, if there were other, earlier examples, did Blackboard get so much attention? How did it so quickly gain so much market share? In part: timing.

Blackboard arrived on the scene in the midst of the Dot Com bubble (and bust) of the late 1990s, where there was an incredible influx of investment into all sorts of online endeavors. Blackboard raised investment from the likes of Pearson, Dell, and AOL. The company went public in 2004. In July 2006 it received the patent for "Internet-based education support system and methods," and the same day it filed a patent infringement lawsuit against its competitor Desire2Learn. That case that was eventually settled in 2009 after the US Patent Office revoked Blackboard's patent claims. Blackboard, its reputation severely damaged in education technology circles by this patent fight, eventually went private, and it was acquired by a private equity firm in 2011. 17 years later,

Blackboard is still here, one of the few remaining survivors in education technology from the Dot Com period.

The Dot Com and AOL references are important because I think it points very much to the technology and business interests that drove Blackboard, and more broadly, it highlights features of the learning management system as we have inherited it today.

The LMS was – is – designed as an Internet portal that connects to the student information system, and much like the old portals of the Dot Com era, much like AOL for example, it cautions you when you try to venture outside of it. "Are you *sure* you want to leave AOL?" "Are you sure you want to leave the VLE?" "Aren't you scared to be on the Web?" "There are strangers and strange ideas out there. Stay within the LMS! Stay within AOL!"

You can access these services *through* your Web browser but they are not really *of* the Web.

I can't really put all the blame here on the shoulders of Blackboard or the technology sector. They sold a product, but schools bought it. And they bought it because these systems matched some of the very traditional visions of how education should work. How education worked offline translated into how courses would work online. What a course looked like. How a course, and the knowledge that was generated and shared therein, began and ended in conjunction with the academic calendar. How each course is a separate entity – one instructor and a roster – hermetically sealed in a walled off online space, much like a walled off classroom.

When I say that the learning management system worked like AOL or other early Internet portals it is also because, for the user, the experience was about access to course-related information through the browser. But on the backend, the LMS connected to the school's student information system. The student information system did not offer a way to open student information or course information to the Internet. It was a closed, proprietary tool. It wasn't about learning. It was about administration. Course enrollment. Scheduling. Grades.

The learning management system built a layer on top of that. Despite all the bells and whistles that have been added since – in Blackboard's case, for example, the acquisition of WebCT and the ability to do video conferencing – the learning management system remains a way to offload the administrative needs of the student information system – roster, grades, attendance for each individual class – to an interface, accessible through the Web, that students and faculty can use.

One of my great ed-tech fears: seeing MOOCs, hailed as the "big new thing" in ed-tech, build their online classes on technologies that look exactly like the LMS. That is: a student signs up for a course. A course that has a beginning date and an end date. Despite the adjective "open," the course is behind a wall. Everything is meant to take place therein. At the end of the course, the student loses access to the material and to any of the content or data they've created. Indeed, the latter is often signed away as part of the Terms of Service. There is one instructor. Maybe two. Maybe some course assistants. They grade. They monitor the forums. The instructors are the center.

The content is the center.

The learner is not the center.

The Web, of course, does not work this way.

The infrastructure of the Web is (or was or is ideally) open. It's built upon a series of open source technologies. Its infrastructure and ethos are open. Open and participatory. The Web allows contributions ostensibly from anyone: the read-write Web. You can point your Web browser to a particular site, and through hyperlinks, you can move through a series of related information and citations. You can build your own site and link your own content to the Web.

I don't think we can overstate how much this has the power to reshape how we teach and learn, and how information, ideas, and people can be connected. The technologies, through links and APIs, enable this; and as such the Web and Internet technologies have enabled a networked learning. This gives us access to an incredible amount of information, yes. But more importantly, the Web enables access to community, to people from whom and with whom we can learn.

If we think about new technologies like the Web as facilitating learning networks and as learners and learning communities as nodes on those networks, we can see a very different "shape," if you will, to education technology than what the learning management system enables.

The Web versus a Wall. Distribution rather than seclusion. Reciprocity rather than recitation.

Nodes and networks need not be forcibly centered around the instructor, for starters. Learners – and we are all learners, not simply those who are formally enrolled in classes – can have say in what they create, how they create it, where they share it, how long they retain it, what it looks like.

They can do this, of course, if they own their own space, their own domain on the Web.

One of the most innovative projects in ed-tech is the Domain of One's Own initiative out of the University of Mary Washington. UMW gives faculty and students their own Web domain. Not simply, as the University of Oregon once gave me, a Web space at the university dot edu slash tilde student name. Their own domain. The university helps them register the domain and hosts it while the students are at the school. Then, when they graduate, they can take it with them. The domain and the content and the data and the learning that all this represents are theirs.

The initiative works alongside an extensive campus-wide blogging program. Many professors maintain their own blogs and assign blogs and other digital projects as part of students' coursework. So instead of writing a term paper than no one but the professor ever sees, the students can display their work on the Web, in public. They can receive feedback from their peers, indeed from the entire Web. Using RSS feeds and tagging, instructors are able to pull in just those blog posts that are related to a particular class into a class website. The students' content can live on their own site and be syndicated to a class hub.

I should note, to assuage any fears about students' privacy, that they are able to run their domains under pseudonyms. Some do.

But many use the opportunity to start building a rich professional portfolio. By owning their own domains, students can learn and demonstrate skills – very desirable skills – in HTML, Web design, and WordPress. They can come to recognize the importance of digital identity – what it means to control and shape it, what it means to own your data.

This question of "owning your data" is incredibly important. When I talk about "owning your data" in terms of education, I often talk about the manila envelope in which my mum saved all my old, analog school stuff. Drawings, stories, report cards, awards. Because of the bounded design of some of the technologies we have adopted, we don't have an opportunity to create a digital equivalent. We lose access to our data. Someone else controls the data. Students are mandated to use certain products – that is, to put the data it, but then find that they cannot get it out.

This lock-in and lockdown is something that the learning management system does really well.

It's something that other technologies now do quite well too.

Wired Magazine tried to argue back in 2010 that "The Web is Dead." "As much as we love the open, unfettered Web," wrote then editor Chris Anderson, "we're abandoning it for simpler, sleeker services that just work. ... Over the past few years, one of the most important shifts in the digital world has been the move from the wide-open Web to semiclosed platforms that use the Internet for transport but not the browser for display."

Around the same time – perhaps not so coincidentally – we started to hear a lot about the potential for "big data," how analytics and algorithms (often extracted from and build on our data) were going to reshape every industry, every field – including education. Most major LMSes, for example, now sell schools analytics packages, using students' interactions with the software to measure and predict things like course completion and retention.

I believe reports of the Web's death, to paraphrase Mark Twain, are greatly exaggerated. Indeed, despite the interests of many technology companies in funneling our activities into applications that are closed off

114

from the Web – without URLs, without syndication, without data portability, often without privacy protections where all our activities are set to be data-mined – the Web remains. It remains a site of great hope and great promise. It remains easily readable, writable, and hackable. And despite the efforts of the Facebooks and the Blackboards of the world, there's a push for a return to the Web, the "indie Web," that many of us fell in love with when we first dialed up to it, when we first escaped AOL.

Today the content we create – we all create, but particularly learners create – is important, even critical I'd suggest to the development of our identities, the protection of our well-being. It is not secure in the hands of startups or big corporations – these companies go away. It is not secure in the hands of schools. Schools are not in the business of long term data storage, and they increasingly outsource their IT to those very startups and big corporations.

We must become the holders of our own data, but not so that we bury all of it away from view. We will want to share it with others on our own terms.

We in education can reclaim the Web and more broadly ed-tech for teaching and learning. But we must reclaim control of the data, content, and knowledge we create. We are not resources to be mined. Learners do not enter our schools and in our libraries to become products for the textbook industry and the testing industry and the technology industry and the VLE industry and the MOOC industry – the ed-tech industry – to profit from.

Ed-tech must be not become an extraction effort, and it increasingly is. The future, I think we'll find, will be a reclamation project. Ed-tech must not be about building digital walls around students and content and courses. We have, thanks to the Web, an opportunity to build connections, build networks, not walls.

Let's move beyond the LMS, back to and forward to an independent Web and let's help our students take full advantage of it.

This talk was delivered on September 5, 2014 to a group at Newcastle University (and was sponsored by NUTELA, a campus digital learning initiative that is unrelated to hazelnut chocolate spread). The original transcript for this talk is available on Hack Education at http://hackeducation.com/2014/09/05/beyond-the-lms-newcastle-university/

WORKS CITED

Chris Anderson and Michael Wolff, "The Web is Dead. Long Live the Internet." *Wired Magazine.* August 17, 2010.

http://www.wired.com/2010/08/ff_webrip/all/

Mark Leibovich, "Blackboard Chalks Up a Breakthrough; Its Educational Software Lets Colleges Put Classes on the Internet." *The Washington Post.* January 4, 1999.

12 THE FUTURE OF ED-TECH IS A RECLAMATION PROJECT

I. DYSTOPIAN FUTURES

Thank you very much for inviting me here to talk to you about the future of digital learning in Alberta – it is an honor and, I admit, a surprise.

See, I'm known for delivering less-than-optimistic assessments about the state of education technology today and for offering caution about the direction in which I see ed-tech heading. Someone once called me "education's Cassandra." But really, it's others' predictions I worry about. I hear their visions for the future of education, and I think "how utterly dystopian!": that in 50 years time we'll only have 10 universities left in the world; that in 15 years time half of the universities (in the US at least) will be bankrupt; that before the end of the century, 70% of today's occupations will be replaced by automation, including the work of librarians and teaching assistants; that public support for education is gone; that precarity and austerity will be the new normal.

As such, I find it challenging to look too positively at the "disruptive innovation" that technology is supposed to enable, in part because I worry about growing inequalities – inequalities, along with other problems, that can never really be resolved with an app or a tablet but that require instead a deeper commitment to democracy.

This is, of course, why education matters so profoundly.

So I've come lately to cite Antonio Gramsci: "I am a pessimist because of intelligence, but an optimist because of will."

But I'm going to will myself to craft a story for you today about education in 2030 that resists that dystopian narrative. I want to project a story for the future where learning technologies support and foster learner control and learner agency. It's a story where students are the subjects not objects when it comes to education and education technology.

It's actually a story we could tell starting today. We have the technology to do so. It is the will that we lack.

II. THE MANILA ENVELOPE

A personal anecdote: a couple of years ago, my mum gave me a large manila envelope full of my old schoolwork – drawings and writings and photos from as far back as preschool. Some projects I remembered; many I did not. Much of the envelope's contents were administrative records: my report cards, various certificates of accomplishment, some ribbons.

That envelope was obviously a low-tech way to collect my school records. One envelope clearly couldn't contain everything I did or everything I made or everything I wrote or everything I learned. It was certainly my mother's curation of "what counts" as my education data. It was a reflection of proud parenting and of schooling in a pre-digital age.

Nevertheless I think the manila envelope is an interesting and an important model – a model with strengths and weaknesses and strange relevancies for us to think about the digital documentation and storage and sharing of education data today.

What happens now that our schoolwork is increasingly "born digital"? What happens to our learning record now that we're recognizing more and more that learning happens beyond the classroom walls, beyond the years of formal schooling?

Is there a virtualized equivalent to my mum's envelope?

(No. There is not.)

But let's imagine. What would or could a virtual manila envelope contain? Grades? Test scores? Attendance records? The pictures a learner has drawn? The poems and essays and book reports she's written? Every assignment she's ever completed – after all, digital storage is so cheap these days. Why not keep everything? A list of every book checked out from the library. Metadata from every educational video watched – all the pauses, rewinds, fast forwards. All that data that we create these days thanks to computer technologies. Every single mouse click on every single piece of software.

"By collecting every click, homework submission, quiz and forum note from tens of thousands of students" – this is how Coursera co-founder Daphne Koller's TED Talk is described – MOOCs have become "a data mine that offers a new way to study learning."

But do students own their own data? Can they study it? Can they control whom it's shared with? Can they export it from Coursera into their own "manila envelope"? As it currently stands – in Coursera as in almost all educational software, no. It's really not your data. You can't get it out. There is no manila envelope.

III. METAPHORS MATTER

OK, I lied. A quick foray into the darker, dystopian side of education data:

Now although I write about education and technology for a living, my formal academic training is in neither area. I'm a literature and language person, and so when I hear MOOCs described as a "data mine," my first thoughts aren't about mathematical models. I think about metaphor. I think about cultural history.

The phrase "data-mining" is quite new – less than 25 or so years old. But prior to that, in the 1960s, statisticians referred to the pouring through data without an a-priori hypothesis as "data-dredging," a practice that then carried a negative connotation.

In that same period, the public grew more and more concerned about data collection and its potential misuse, particularly with regards to violations of privacy. Indeed, as banking, healthcare, and government services were becoming increasingly computerized, the 1960s and 1970s saw the passing of several laws – many still on the books – addressing the collection, storage, and sale of people's personal data. This includes in the United States FERPA, the Family Educational Rights and Privacy Act, the law that governs the privacy of students' education records.

Data-dredging. Data-mining. Technological processes, sure, but political processes too. And really interesting metaphors.

Dredging data conjures up the image of searching through a large, fluid pool of information. Dredging up information from the bottom, information that's been buried, that's otherwise inaccessible. And, to press the metaphor: dredging in the physical world is largely recognized to disturb the ecosystem and to leave behind toxic chemicals.

Mining data might suggest a more targeted resource extraction than dredging data. It certainly suggests a more lucrative one. But we don't always talk about the potential toxic results.

"Data is the new oil," headlines proclaim. "Data is just like crude," says the market analyst. "It's valuable, but if unrefined it cannot really be used. It has to be changed into gas, plastic, chemicals, etc., to create a valuable entity that drives profitable activity; so must data be broken down, analyzed for it to have value."

"Data is the new oil," says the investor, urging startups to locate and mine resources currently untapped

"Data is the new oil," says The World Economic Forum. "In practical terms, a person's data could be equivalent to their 'money.'"

I am not sure how much these natural resource extraction metaphors resonate here in Alberta. They resonate for me. I was born in Wyoming, where the mining industry drives the economy. I understand firsthand the cycles of boom and bust. Wyoming is also the site of the Teapot Dome scandal, which before Watergate, was the biggest scandal in the history of the US government. The Teapot Dome Scandal occurred in the 1920s when the Warren G. Harding administration gave private companies opportunities to mine public lands in Wyoming without going through the proper bidding process.

So when I hear "data is the new oil," I think about this language, this history, the sorts of relationships that have long been forged between government and corporate entities. Public resources, private profits. And what that means for prosperity, for growth, for sustainability.

I get it: to call data "the new oil" is particularly resonant in our energy-hungry and fossil-fuel reliant economy. And for what it's worth, some data scientists have pushed back on the "oil" metaphor. Jer Thorp, an educator and the former data artist in residence at *The New York Times* has argued that the "data is the new oil" metaphor, when wielded uncritically, is deeply flawed. Data isn't something that lies beneath the surface, just waiting to be extracted. Thorp writes,

"Perhaps the 'data as oil' idea can foster some much-needed criticality. Our experience with oil has been fraught; fortunes made have been balanced with dwindling resources, bloody mercenary conflicts, and a terrifying climate crisis. If we are indeed making the first steps into economic terrain that will be as transformative (and possibly as risky) as that of the petroleum industry, foresight will be key. We have already seen 'data spills' happen (when large amounts of personal data are inadvertently leaked). Will it be much longer until we see dangerous data drilling practices? Or until we start to see long term effects from 'data pollution'?

One of the places where we'll have to tread most carefully ... is in the realm of personal data. A great deal of the profit that is being made right now in the data world is being made through the use of human-generated information. Our browsing habits, our conversations with friends, our movements and location – all of these things are being monetized. This is deeply human data, though very often it is not treated as such. Here, perhaps we can invoke a comparison to fossil fuel in a useful way: where oil is composed of the compressed bodies of long-dead micro-organisms, this personal data is made from the compressed fragments of our personal lives. It is a dense condensate of our human experience."

If we are to embrace the "the new oil" metaphor, Thorp insists that we do so critically and ethically, thinking through all the implications, and not merely those implications that have the "mining" executives rubbing their hands together in glee, promising the innovations while anticipating the profits.

What does it mean to talk about student data using this metaphor "the new oil"? The promised innovation in this case: if we can just mine enough student data, we will uncover the secret about how best to teach and learn. Again, how does this metaphor color the way we build technologies, devise policies?

Would we talk about student data this same way, would we feel entitled to access and analyze student data the same way if we thought of it more like that manila envelope?

To tell a brighter story about the future of ed-tech, I do think we will need to talk about student data in a different way, with different metaphors and with a different politic. I want to encourage the building of technologies that see students' lives and learning not as a resource to be extracted but as something they themselves can control and cultivate.

IV. "HOSTED LIFEBITS"

But to gesture to the future, I want to turn to the past: to seven years ago when Jon Udell, a Microsoft researcher who's long explored how non-engineers can use Internet technologies in new and empowering ways, began arguing for something he called "hosted lifebits" – a way for us to consolidate and control our own data in our own repositories. Manila envelopes perhaps, but Internet-enabled.

"Lifebits" – that word is really powerful, I think, and it helps us recognize that all this data we're creating – intentionally and unintentionally – is us. Bits and bytes of data, sure, but bits and pieces of our lives. Mining that sounds less appealing, I'd argue, than simply mining "data."

The "lifebits" idea actually comes from another Microsoft researcher, Gordon Bell, who undertook a project to build a personal archive of all the digital assets related to his life, and going forward, to capture, in close to real time, all the digitalia he created.

For Udell, adding the adjective "hosted" to Bell's concept means that a repository of "lifebits" would be stored in the cloud where it could interact with other repositories and other people.

Udell wrote in a blog post in 2007, "Today my digital assets are spread out all over the place. Some are on various websites that I control, and a lot more that I don't. Others are on various local hard disks that I control, and a lot more that I don't. It's become really clear to me that I'd be willing to pay for the service of consolidating all this stuff, syndicating it to wherever it's needed, and guaranteeing its availability throughout – and indeed beyond – my lifetime.

The scenario, as I've been painting it in conversations with friends and associates, begins at childbirth. In addition to a social security number, everyone gets a handle to a chunk of managed storage. How that's coordinated by public- and private-sector entities is an open question, but here's how it plays out from the individual's point of view."

Udell then imagines what it might mean to collect all of one's important data from grade school, high school, college and work – to have the ability to turn this into a portfolio – for posterity, for personal reflection, and for professional display on the Web:

> Grade 3
>
> Your teacher assigns a report that will be published in your e-portfolio, which is a website managed by the school. Your parents tell you to write the report, and publish it into your space. Then they release it to the school's content management system. A couple of years later the school switches to a new system and breaks all the old URLs. But the original version remains accessible throughout your parents' lives, and yours, and even your kids'.
>
> Grade 8
>
> On the class trip to Washington, DC, you take a batch of digital photos. You want to share them on MySpace, so you do, but not directly, because MySpace isn't really your space. So you upload the photos to the place that really is your space, where they'll be permanently and reliably available, then you syndicate them into MySpace for the social effects that happen there.
>
> Grade 11
>
> You're applying to colleges. You publish your essay into your space, then syndicate it to the common application service. The essay points to supporting evidence – your e-portfolio, recommendations – which are also ... permanently recorded in your space.
>
> And so on ...

"Hosted lifebits." The idea, again, is that we each would have the ability – at the very least access to the technology or to a service – to maintain our own data repository for ourselves but also for our offspring. Parents would manage their children's repositories and then hand the keys over to them when they're grown; adults in turn would manage their repositories and then hand them over to their children or perhaps will them to an archive or institution when they die.

The links to the lifebits don't rot; the data doesn't disappear.

If your education-related lifebits are in your own repository, you are able to audit your education record – to correct incorrect data, to run your own analyses of the things that are meaningful to you as a learner.

You have the ability to control who has access to your lifebits. This is absolutely crucial. With lifebits, you opt in, rather than as now, where we have to opt *out* of analytics and algorithms. You can decide what is shared publicly or shared privately or what is not shared at all.

You have the technology to help you remember. You retain the ability – and the right – to delete, to forget.

"The technical aspects are somewhat challenging," Udell wrote in 2007, "but the social and business aspects are even more challenging."

V. A DOMAIN OF ONE'S OWN

Today, the technical aspects are somewhat less challenging. There are ways to get data in and out of software, although many continue to make it incredibly difficult to do so. There's still a lack of interoperability. There are still proprietary formats. But it is technically feasible to create systems where our data is distributed across our own repositories, rather than centralized into various applications.

The obstacles, as Udell rightly noted, remain the business models that particularly in educational software compel companies to collect and retain data in a silo. In *their* silo. There they can mine student data, often selling the insights they can glean back to schools.

The obstacles to "hosted lifebits" stem too from the cultural expectations that schools have for software – software often designed to the meet the needs of administrators rather than learners or their parents.

These technological silos work too because we still view each classroom as a closed entity, because we view each subject or discipline as atomistic and distinct. Closed. Centralized. Control in the hands of administrators, teachers, IT but rarely in the hands of learners.

As such it's no surprise that the learning management system has dominated ed-tech for the last 20+ years – again, the words we use here matter: "learning" "management" "system." The LMS has profoundly shaped how schools interact with the Internet, I'd argue. The LMS is a piece of administrative software that pretends to address questions about teaching and learning, often circumscribing pedagogical possibilities, quite frankly. The LMS works as an Internet portal to the student information system, and much like the old portals of the AOL era, cautions you when you try to venture outside of it. You can access the LMS through your web browser but it is not *of* the Web.

And at the end of each semester or school year students typically lose access to their course materials – to the syllabus, the readings, the quizzes, the discussion posts. There is no way for students to export all their data.

There is no manila envelope.

It doesn't have to be like this.

One alternative path is being forged by a small team at the liberal arts college University of Mary Washington, which offers what I think is one the most innovative ed-tech initiatives: A Domain of One's Own.

Students and faculty at the University of Mary Washington get their own domain. It isn't simply Web space on the university servers, a dot edu with a slash tilde namespace. The Domain of One's Own initiative gives students and faculty their *own* URL: www dot whomever they might be or want to be dot com. The university pays for the domain registration and the hosting while the students are enrolled, and when they graduate, the domain and the data goes with them. It's theirs.

Their own domain. Again, the word matters here. Students have their own space on the Web. A space for a blog or multiple blogs. A digital portfolio for their academic work that can become a professional portfolio as well. A place to store their digital stuff in the cloud.

Moreover, a lesson on the technologies that underpin the Web. HTML. CSS. RSS.

It's not quite "hosted lifebits," but it's a solid step in that direction. The initiative represents a kind of open learning – learning *on* the Web and *with* the Web, learning that is *of* the Web. "Domain of One's Own" offers a resistance to the silos of the learning management system and to the student as a data mine. It highlights the importance of learner agency, of learning in public, of learning together, of control over one's digital identity and over one's educational data, and the increasing importance of digital literacies.

VI. ED-TECH AS A RECLAMATION PROJECT

I think one of the most powerful learning technologies humans have ever created is the World Wide Web. Its power doesn't lie simply in all the "content." We get too distracted by that. The power of the Web lies in the human connections, in our intellectual and social networks. That schools block the Web and filter the Web and discourage its usage is a terrible shame. That schools fail to help students learn about how the Web works and how they will likely form and perform some digital identity there is a terrible missed opportunity.

Wired Magazine tried to argue back in 2010 that "The Web is Dead." "As much as we love the open, unfettered Web," wrote then editor Chris Anderson, "we're abandoning it for simpler, sleeker services that just work. ... Over the past few years, one of the most important shifts in the digital world has been the move from the wide-open Web to semiclosed platforms that use the Internet for transport but not the browser for display."

But reports of the Web's death, to paraphrase Mark Twain, are greatly exaggerated. Indeed, despite the interests of many technology companies in funneling our activities into applications that are closed off from the Web – without URLs, without syndication, without data portability, often without privacy protections where all our activities are set to be data-mined – the Web remains. It remains a site of great hope and great promise. It remains easily readable, writable, and hackable. And despite the efforts of the Facebooks and the Blackboards of the world, there's a push for a return to the Web, the "indie Web," many of us fell in love with when we first dialed up to it, when we first escaped AOL.

Today the content we create – we all create, but particularly learners create – is important, even critical I'd suggest to the development of our identities, the protection of our well-being. It is not secure in the hands of startups or big corporations – these companies go away. It is not secure in the hands of schools. Schools are not in the business of long term data storage, and they increasingly outsource their IT to those very startups and big corporations. We must become the holders of our own data, but not so that we bury all of it away from view. We will want to share it with others on our own terms.

We can reclaim the Web and more broadly ed-tech for teaching and learning. But we must reclaim control of the data, content, and knowledge we create. We are not resources to be mined. Learners do not enter our schools and in our libraries to become products for the textbook industry and the testing industry and the technology industry and the ed-tech industry to profit from.

Ed-tech must be not become an extraction effort, and it increasingly is. The future, I think we'll find, will be a reclamation project. Let's start now to take ed-tech back.

This keynote was delivered at the Alberta Digital Learning Forum on May 22, 2014 in Calgary, Alberta. The original transcript is available on Hack Education at http://hackeducation.com/2014/05/22/alberta-digital-learning-forum/

WORKS CITED

Chris Anderson and Michael Wolff, "The Web is Dead. Long Live the Internet." *Wired Magazine.* August 17, 2010. http://www.wired.com/2010/08/ff_webrip/all/

Daphne Koller, "What We're Learning From Online Education." TED. http://www.ted.com/talks/daphne_koller_what_we_re_learning_from_online_education

Jon Udell, "Hosted Lifebits." May 22, 2007. http://blog.jonudell.net/2007/05/22/hosted-lifebits/

Jer Thorp, "Big Data is Not the New Oil." *Harvard Business Review.* November 30, 2012. https://hbr.org/2012/11/data-humans-and-the-new-oil/

World Economic Forum, "Personal Data: The Emergence of a New Asset Class." January 2011.
http://www3.weforum.org/docs/WEF_ITTC_PersonalDataNewAsset_Report_2011.pdf

13 BENEATH THE COBBLESTONES: A DOMAIN OF ONE'S OWN

"What technologies have you seen lately that you like?" people always ask me. It's a trick question, I reckon. "What in ed-tech is exciting? What in ed-tech innovative?" These questions make me sigh. Heavily.

But I am on record – several times in several places – calling "Domain of One's Own" one of the most important and innovative initiatives in ed-tech today. The responses I get to such an assertion are always revealing.

Oh sure, I get plenty of nods and shouts that "hell yeah, Jim Groom rocks!" (And he does. and his team rocks even more.)

But then too, I get a fair amount of pushback. People question, "What the hell is 'Domain of One's Own'?" Or "Is it like that *Seinfeld* episode?" Or "I've never heard of it. Has *Techcrunch* written about it?" Or more commonly, "Why is having a blog a big deal?" Or "My university gave us Web space back in 1994."

Or, in a nutshell I suppose: "I don't get it. How is it innovative?"

I. INNOVATION

What's different, what's special about the "Domain of One's Own" project?

It isn't simply "a blog." It isn't simply slash your user name on the university's dot edu.

The initiative represents a kind of open learning – learning *on* the Web and *with* the Web, learning that is *of* the Web – and all along the way, "Domain of One's Own" offers a resistance to the silos of the traditional learning management system and of traditional academic disciplines.

It highlights the importance of learner agency, learning in public, control over one's digital identity, and the increasing importance of Web literacies.

But I recognize that the "Domain of One's Own" initiative does, in many ways, run counter to how the tech industry and the ed-tech industry today define and market "innovation" and how in turn we teachers and students, we consumers, we "users" are meant to view and admire such developments.

Google Glass – *that's* innovative. Google's self-driving car – *that's* innovative. These aren't ed-tech products, of course. And Google Glass and Google's self-driving car – for the time being, at least – are not being heavily marketed to schools, unlike Google Apps for Education, Google Course Builder, Google Chrome, Google Chromebooks, Google Hangouts, Google Helpouts, Android tablets, YouTube, Google Books, Google MOOCs, Google Scholar, and so on.

We can probably debate whether or not the Google products pushed on schools are really *that* innovative. And perhaps – and sadly – that's what we've come to expect from ed-tech: it is acceptably behind-the-curve.

Yet unlike many technologies that are specifically geared towards classrooms, Google doesn't really suffer from its association with ed-tech, does it? Instead, it's credited with bringing a long-overdue technical boost to schools. And it's free!

Of course, you could argue that Google does have an education-oriented mission of sorts: "to organize the world's information and make it universally accessible and useful."

And yet in undertaking this mission, let's be clear, Google's "innovation" is not associated that closely with educational institutions – be they libraries or universities or K–12 schools. In other words, the company positions its products as a benefit *for* educational institutions, but Google is not really *of* educational institutions. Google clearly brands itself as a tech innovation, a Silicon Valley innovation, even though you could argue it's surely a Stanford University-born one.

You could argue too that as Google has grown, so too have the implications of its efforts to "organize the world's information." These implications are political. Economic. Technological. Scientific. Cultural. And they are global.

Google looks less and less like a library card catalog, if you will, that helps us find what we're searching for on the Web. That's particularly true in light of its some of its most recent acquisitions: a company that builds military robots, a company that manufactures solar-powered drones, and one that makes Internet-connected thermostats and smoke alarms, for example.

No doubt, these are new ways, new products that use "the world's information." Often, that use our information.

We're told this exchange – this extraction, if you will – fosters innovation.

Google Glass and Google's self-driving car are initiatives of the company's mysterious laboratory Google X. Although Google prides itself (and brands itself) as being an "innovative" company, Google X is supposedly even more ambitious. The work of Google X involves technology "moon shots" as CEO and co-founder Larry Page calls them.

Here's how an article in *Bloomberg Businessweek* describes the lab, a gentle reminder of the military history from which computer research emerged:

"Google X seeks to be an heir to the classic research labs, such as the Manhattan Project, which created the first atomic bomb, and Bletchley Park, where code breakers cracked German ciphers and gave birth to modern cryptography. ... 'Google believes in and enables us to do things that wouldn't be possible in academia,' says Chris Urmson, a former assistant research professor at Carnegie Mellon [and now the head of the self-driving car project]."

"Things that wouldn't be possible in academia."

Perhaps because academia doesn't have the resources. Perhaps because of a focus (real or perceived) on theoretical, rather than applied research. Perhaps because of a disregard or distaste for the commercial. Perhaps because academia – some parts of it at least, and some institutions – likes to minimize or ignore or distance itself from its connections to the development of war technologies – as does the current computer industry, no doubt. Perhaps because academia doesn't do that good a job at promoting its scholarship to the public – you know, "in organizing the world's information and making it universally accessible and useful." Perhaps because academia doesn't do a good job of hyping its achievements. Perhaps because academia doesn't employ a large number of PR representatives. And perhaps because innovation is increasingly defined as something that comes from industry and not the university, something that is fostered in the private sector and not the public.

Much of what happens at Google X is secret, but among its other research projects we do know of: Google Contact Lenses, an experiment to see if tiny sensors on contact lenses can offer a non-intrusive way to monitor diabetics' glucose levels. Project Loon, an experiment to use high altitude balloons to deliver Internet to people in remote areas. And Google Brain, a vast computer simulation of the human brain, a "neural network" of thousands of connected computer processors. "Deep Learning" this is called.

A couple of names of those who've worked at Google X in addition to Google co-founder Sergey Brin: Sebastian Thrun. Andrew Ng

Sebastian Thrun, one of the creators of Google's self-driving car, who also happens to be a Stanford artificial intelligence professor, who also happens to be the co-founder of Udacity, an online education startup.

Andrew Ng, one of the researchers on Google Brain, who also happens to be a Stanford artificial intelligence professor, who also happens to be the co-founder of Coursera, another online education startup.

Now I'm disinclined to talk to you this afternoon about MOOCs. Dammit, I'm here to talk about the "Domain of One's Own"! And God knows, we've spilled enough ink on the topic of MOOCs over the course of the last eighteen months or so. But MOOCs are a subtext of this talk nonetheless.

It's possible Thrun and Ng's work at Google X might just be an inconsequential line on their CVs – the ties between Stanford and Google ain't no big thing.

But I think this connection between Google X and MOOCs is pretty noteworthy. It points towards one vision for the future of teaching and learning with technology, one vision of what happens to the content we create as teachers and learners, one vision of who owns and controls all the data.

It's also interesting to consider why some people balk at a "Domain of One's Own" being innovative and yet clamor over MOOCs as the greatest and newest thing education has ever seen.

And I'll add too, it is striking to me – it's part of the motivation for my writing a book on the history of automation in education – that two of the leading scientists at Google X, two of the leading scientists in the field of artificial intelligence and artificial intelligence at scale have opted to launch companies that purport to address developing human intelligence, through instruction and content delivery at scale.

II. SCALE

MOOCs as ideology. Google as ideology. "Scale" as ideology.

Scale is important to tech companies like Google and their global reach. It's important in their economic impact and in the way that economic growth – particularly venture capital funded growth – gets framed.

"Scale" is important in the breadth of tech companies' offerings (particularly in the case of Google, which is hardly just a search engine anymore, although it does remain, if you judge it by its revenues, an advertising company).

"Scale" is important as we see the number of sectors being transformed (or threatened with transformation) by new technologies, as media studies professor Siva Vaidhyanathan has described it in his book *The Googlization of Everything*.

"Scale" is important too in how many of these new technologies work – how they work practically and how they work ideologically. By that I mean that "scale" and this business-technological lens is increasingly framing the way we view the world, so much so that we must ask "Does it scale?" about every idea or initiative, good or bad.

And when we ask "Does it scale?" we often mean, "Can we replicate this across systems in an orderly, standardized way thanks to Internet connectivity and proprietary software solutions and venture capital?" Or we mean "Is this idea 'the next Google'?"

Our technological world necessitates thinking in and working in and expanding at scale. Or that's the message from the tech and business sector at least: scale is necessary; technological progress demands it.

And here again, we can see that just as the "Domain of One's Own" does not fit in an industry-oriented definition of "innovation," nor does it neatly fit into this view of "scale" either – even as we see the project spread from the University of Mary Washington to Emory University and elsewhere. The "Domain of One's Own" initiative grows through the hard work of community-building and capacity-building, not simply through technical replication.

But Google. Google scales.

"Scale" is important to all of Google's efforts. Google works, of course, at "Web scale," and scale is, if nothing else, important in the size and distribution of Google's infrastructure, its server farms.

Every time you type a word or phrase into Google's search box, that query hits between 700 and 1000 separate computers. These machines scan Google's indexes of the Web and generate about 5 million search results, delivered back to you in .16 seconds.

That's the infrastructure for *one* search. So it's hard perhaps to fathom the complexity and, well, the scale involved in *all* the search queries Google handles.

And more: it's hard to imagine the complexity and scale involved across all the products and services Google offers, all of which are now covered by one Terms of Service agreement – your data and your profile shared across them all. What you search for on Google. Your Gmail. Your Google Calendar plans. Your friends on Google+. What you've bought with Google Wallet. What you've downloaded from Google Play. What you've watched on YouTube. Where you head on Google Maps. Where you carry your Android. What you spy with Google Glass.

So much data.

III. DATA

We are all creating mind-bogglingly vast amounts of data, in increasing volume, speed, and complexity. In 2012, IBM pegged this at about 2.5 quintillion bytes of data created every day. No doubt that figure has only increased in the past two years.

This is, of course, what folks call "big data." Numbers too big for your Casio calculator. Numbers too big for your Excel spreadsheet. And this is what many entrepreneurs, technologists, technocrats, politicians, venture capitalists, and quants are quite giddy about. Big data – capturing it, processing it, analyzing it – all of which will purportedly bring about more innovation. More innovation in education. More innovation in education at scale even.

Much of this data explosion comes from various types of sensors. Indeed the number of Internet-connected devices in US homes today now outnumbers the number of people in the country itself. Devices like the Nest thermostat that Google recently acquired.

But plenty of this data is human-generated – if not specifically as what we call "user-generated content" then as "data-exhaust," that is all sorts of metadata that many of us are often quite unaware that we're creating.

Of course, the general public probably is a bit more aware of metadata now, thanks to the revelations last summer of Edward Snowden, the former CIA analyst who disclosed the vast surveillance efforts of the National Security Agency: the collection of massive amounts of data from telephone and technology companies. "Email, videos, photos, voice-over-IP chats, file transfers, social networking details, and more" siphoned from Apple, Google, Facebook, Microsoft, Yahoo, Skype, AOL, World of Warcraft, Angry Birds and so on. Encryption undermined. Malware spread. Our social connections mapped. Warrantless spying by governments – not just on suspected terrorists, but on all of us.

As privacy researcher and activist Chris Soghoian quipped on Twitter, Google has built the greatest global surveillance system. It's no surprise that the NSA has sought to use it too.

Google knows a lot about us. What we search for. Who we email. And when. Where we live. Where we're going. What we watch. What we write. What we read. What we buy.

It mines this data purportedly to offer us better products and services and, of course, to sell ads.

And again, here is where a "Domain of One's Own" runs counter to what is a dominant trend in technology today, particularly a growing trend in education whereby all this data and all this metadata will be used to "personalize education."

A "Domain of One's Own" asks us to consider the infrastructure. It asks us to understand the Web and our place on it. It asks to us to pay attention to the content we create as teachers and as students and to weigh where it best resides – who has access to it, and for how long.

It prompts us to ask "what data are we creating" as learners and "who owns it." Who tracks us. Who profits.

As our worlds become increasingly mediated by computing machines, we're encouraged to hand over more details of our lives, more data to Google (and to other technology companies, of course.)

Most of us think little about this. We shrug. We agree to the Terms of Service without reading them, often meaning we've agreed to hand over our data, to give up control over what's done with it. We acquiesce more and more of our privacy. In doing so, we're assured, technology will give us access to better stuff, to more "innovation."

IV. MAGIC

As Arthur C. Clarke once famously said "any sufficiently advanced technology is indistinguishable from magic."

Technology companies benefit when we think this is all magic. There is little incentive for them to equip us with the critical and the technical capacities to run our own servers, to build our own applications, to use and contribute to open source software, to claim our place on the open Web, and ultimately to challenge their business models. Because let's be clear: for many companies, theirs is a business model predicated on monetizing the content and the data we create.

A "Domain of One's Own" builds literacies so that the technology of the Web *is* distinguishable from magic, so those who understand how to manipulate its symbols are not high priests or magicians, so that carving out and operating your own little piece on the Web is manageable not magic. From there perhaps teachers and students will feel empowered to explore more of technology's terrain, so they feel empowered even to resist its "Googlization."

One quick aside about "magic" because I'm a folklorist by training, and I don't want to dismiss or belittle a belief in wonder. Nor do I want us to move away from a world of wonder towards a world of technocracy, to simply reduce what we do and what we make to terms like "user-generated content" or "personal data" or "data exhaust" or "code." How cold and empty these sound. Love letters reduced to a status update, love songs, their associated metadata. Human communication as a transaction, not an expression.

I think we've convinced ourselves that we've wrested the Internet away from its military origins to do just that, to make a space for poetic self-expression, to make a space for self-directed learning. But I'm not really certain we have been successful. In fact, I'm deeply pessimistic about the path that technology, particularly education technology, is taking.

"I am a pessimist," to quote Antonio Gramsci, "because of intelligence, but an optimist because of will."

I am a skeptic about much of ed-tech because I am a critic of late capitalism, of imperialism, of militarism and surveillance. I think we err when we ignore or forget the role that education and that technology play therein.

I do try to be an optimist. Those of working in education are by necessity, Gardner Campbell has argued. As he wrote last year, "It seems to me that educators, no matter how skeptical their views (skepticism is necessary but not sufficient for an inquiring mind), are implicitly committed to optimism. Otherwise, why learn? and why teach?"

Those of us who work in education believe in ideas, to be sure. We believe in knowledge. We believe, I'd add too, that through collective contemplation, intellectual reciprocity, and deliberate and wise action, the future can be better. But mostly, I think, educators are optimists because we believe in people.

I'm here today speaking to you because of people. Oh sure, I'm here because I do own my own domain. I've leveraged the website I control to tell stories about education and technology, stories that are often very different than those promoted by the business and tech industries, from those promoted by education as well.

But I mean before that. Before I bought the www dot hackeducation dot com domain. Before I bought www dot audrey watters dot com. Way before. A decade ago.

A decade ago I was a grad student, working on my PhD in comparative literature. I didn't start a blog then to talk about academia. Rather, my husband had been diagnosed with liver cancer. He was dying. I was trying to balance care taking him and our 12-year-old son. I was losing my world; I was losing my shit. I was trying to still teach classes. I was supposed to be writing a dissertation.

Instead, I wrote a blog.

These were the early days of academic blogging, when there appeared to be very little support for the sorts of public scholarship that we see now via blogs. Many of us wrote under pseudonyms, uncertain if as graduate students or junior faculty, it was safe for us to be engaged in these public discussions under our real names.

What I found online was not just intellectual camaraderie. I found an incredible community who supported me during my most difficult times in ways that those on my campus never did.

One of those people was David Morgen. I consider him a dear friend and an amazing colleague, even though neither of us is doing now what we thought we'd be doing in academia a decade ago. And even though, until yesterday, we'd never actually met face-to-face.

And that, if anything, is what's magical about technology.

Not how Google can mount a tiny camera onto some plastic eyeglasses. Not how all the data it's collected from its Google Maps project can now be used to help power an autonomous vehicle. Not spam filters on emails. Not collaborative editing of documents. Not technology's business models. Not its political and economic powers. Not the obfuscation of these.

What's magic: the ability to connect to other people – and connect in deeply meaningful ways – even though separated by physical space.

V. RESISTANCE

Of course, Internet companies like Google love it that we love that capability to connect us. That's the stuff of TV ads. Talking to grandparents and grandchildren and astronauts via Google Hangouts. Real tearjerkers.

This desire for human connection – not simply the colder and more technical term "communication" – is perhaps our weak spot, where these companies can so easily strike us, where they can so readily convince us to give up control of our data, our content, our digital identity, to trust them, to let them focus on the technology while we non-technologists focus on the rest.

Perhaps it's what makes education so susceptible to this messaging too – learning can be a moment of such vulnerability and such powerful connection.

But I'd argue too that this desire for connection is just as easily our strength as we grow weary of an emphasis on scaling the technology and scaling the business at the expense of our lives, our data.

We will, I hope – again, this is why I believe "A Domain of One's Own" is so important and so innovative – learn to seize these tools and build something for ourselves. One path forward perhaps, with a nod to Donna Haraway: cyborgs.

"The main trouble with cyborgs," she reminds us, "is that they are the illegitimate offspring of militarism and patriarchal capitalism, not to mention state socialism. But illegitimate offspring are often exceedingly unfaithful to their origins."

A "Domain of One's Own" is a cyborg tactic, I reckon. Kin to the learning management system. Kin to Web 2.0. But unfaithful and subversive to today's Internet technologies and today's educational technologies, connected as these are, as Haraway's manifesto reminds us, to command-control-communication-intelligence.

A cyborg tactic, an "illegitimate offspring," the "Domain of One's Own" is fiercely disloyal to the LMS. Jim Groom and his team at the University of Mary Washington always make that incredibly clear. And I hope eventually too, we'll become fiercely disloyal to Google as well.

The "Domain of One's Own" initiative prompts us to not just own our own domain – our own space on the Web – but to consider how we might need to reclaim bits and pieces that have already been extracted from us.

It prompts us think critically about what our digital identity looks like, who controls it, who owns our data, who tracks it, who's making money from it. It equips us to ask questions – technical questions and philosophical questions and economic questions and political questions about and for ourselves, our communities, our practices, knowing that we have a stake as actors and not just as objects of technology, as actors and not just objects of education technology.

Graffiti from May '68 in Paris pronounced "Beneath the cobblestones, the beach." I know it's hokey to invoke situationist phrases. I realize that the hot new thing, if you're to invoke French analysis of the political economy, would be to cite Thomas Piketty. But damn, I love that situationist phrase. It's so punk rock – the idea that if we dig under the infrastructure of society, we'll find something beautiful. The idea that in our hands, this infrastructure – quite frankly – becomes a weapon.

And that's how we resist Google, how we resist the tech industry writ large. And that's why a "Domain of One's Own" matters, that's why it's incredibly innovative – because it's so wickedly subversive to the whole notion of tech and ed-tech "innovation."

This keynote was delivered at the Domain of One's Own Incubator at Emory University in Atlanta, Georgia on April 25, 2014. The original transcript is available on Hack Education at http://hackeducation.com/2014/04/25/domain-of-ones-own-incubator-emory/

WORKS CITED

Gardner Campbell, "Optimism." September 25, 2013. http://www.gardnercampbell.net/blog1/?p=2151

Glenn Greenwald and Ewen MacAskill, "NSA Prism program taps in to user data of Apple, Google and others." *The Guardian.* June 7, 2013. http://www.theguardian.com/world/2013/jun/06/us-tech-giants-nsa-data

Donna Haraway, "A Cyborg Manifesto: Science, Technology, and Socialist-Feminism in the Late Twentieth Century." *Simians, Cyborgs and Women: The Reinvention of Nature.* Routledge, 1991.

Brad Stone, "Inside Google's Secret Lab." *Bloomberg Businessweek.* May 22, 2013. http://www.businessweek.com/articles/2013-05-22/inside-googles-secret-lab

Siva Vaidhyanathan, *The Googlization of Everything (And Why We Should*

Worry). University of California Press, 2011.

14 CONVIVIAL TOOLS IN AN AGE OF SURVEILLANCE

I'm very excited and honored to be here to talk to you today, in part because obviously that's what you're supposed to say when you're invited to speak at a university. Truthfully, I'm stoked because I'm reaching the end of what has been a very long year of speaking engagements.

Initially, I had planned to spend 2014 working on a book called *Teaching Machines*. I'm absolutely fascinated by the history of education technology – its development as an industry and a field of study, its connection to scientific management and educational psychology and Americans' ongoing fears and fascinations with automation.

I call myself a freelance education writer. But I've spent the year traveling around the world acting more like an education speaker.

I don't really fit in in the education technology speaking circuit. I mean, first off, I'm a woman. Second, I don't tend to talk about ed-tech revolution and disruptive innovation unless it's to critique and challenge those phrases. I don't give ed-tech pep talks, where you leave the room with a list of 300 new apps you can use in your classroom. Third, I'm not selling a product, not selling consulting services, and because I've spent so much time this year traveling and speaking, I'm still not selling a book. And I don't have a shtick. I don't have a script. There isn't actually a TED Talk that you can watch and see almost 100% word-for-word what I'm going to say over the course of a keynote.

That's what you do, I'm told. You write a talk. You give that talk again and again and again and again. You hone your delivery. You hone your jokes; perhaps you localize them.

I do it wrong. I try to write something new each time I talk. I use the opportunity of a public speaking engagement to spend some time crafting

138

An argument, which I do write out in advance to deliver to each audience.

Somewhere along the way – mid-September, I guess – I realized that, while I did not finish writing *Teaching Machines* this year, I did actually write tens of thousands of words on ed-tech. I've got a couple more talks scheduled, but by the end of 2014, I will have delivered over fourteen presentations. That's fourteen chapters. Why, that's a book! So I've decided that I'm going to collect all the talks I've written and self-publish them.

It's like I did everything backwards: I did the book tour, and then I published the book.

Of course, once I had this great idea, once I decided to publish my talks as a book, I had to spend some time thinking about how they'd be ordered and grouped. I didn't want to simply present them in chronological order: what I said in January. Then what I said in February. Then what I said in March. So I needed to group my talks into sections, by theme.

And then I realized too that, if I was going to publish my talks as a book, I need to think a bit more strategically about what I wanted to say in my final few presentations.

See, I wanted to the book to have an arc. You have to have an arc.

If you're familiar with my work, you know that I'm pretty critical of the shape that education technology takes, has taken, is taking. Perhaps it's because I describe myself as a "recovering academic," I get a lot of snarls in response to my criticism, that all I know how to do is "what grad students do" and that's "criticize." I hear this a lot, particularly from entrepreneurs who proudly proclaim that they "build" while I "tear things down."

I think that's bullshit, frankly – often a cheap anti-intellectualism that posits markets as making and scholars as destructive.

Nevertheless as I've weighed how I'd pull together my 2014 "book tour" into an actual book, I figured, heck, I should probably not send my readers in the final chapters into a downward spiral of education technology despair. I live there, people, and it's gloomy. So I figured I should find something, some way to wrap things up – not necessarily on an "up" note, but on an activist note, on a note that says that we can resist some of the dominant narratives about what education technology can or should do.

"Say something positive about ed-tech, Audrey." Easier said than done. But when I was asked to give a title and an abstract for this talk today, I decided to try.

Or at least, what I want to talk about today is how we can push back on the hype surrounding ed-tech disruption and revolution, how we can ask questions about whose revolution this might be – to what end, for whose benefit – and how we can, should, must begin to talk more seriously about education technologies that are not build upon control and surveillance. We must think about education technologies in informal learning settings, and not simply in institutional ones. We need to talk about ed-tech and social justice, and not kid ourselves for a minute that Silicon Valley is going to get us there.

So in doing so, I decided to invoke in the title of this talk Ivan Illich's notion of "convivial tools."

The phrase comes from his 1973 book *Tools for Conviviality*, published just two years after the book he's probably best known for, *Deschooling Society*.

These are just two of a number of very interesting, progressive if not radical texts about education from roughly the same period: Paul Goodman's *Compulsory Mis-education* (1964). Jonathan Kozol's *Death at an Early Age* (1967). Neil Postman's *Teaching as a Subversive Activity* (1969). Paulo Freire's *Pedagogy of the Oppressed* (first published in Portuguese in 1968 and in English in 1970). Everett Reimer's *School is Dead* (1971).

These books (loosely) share a diagnosis: that our education system is controlling, exploitative, imperialist; that despite all our talk about democratization and opportunity, school often neatly reinforces the hierarchies of our socio-economic world – categorizations based on race and class and gender and nationality.

(Let me stress "gender" there. I can't help but notice that this list, much like the list of those on the education speaking circuit today, is full of men.)

During roughly the same period as the publication of these books challenging traditional education and traditional schooling, there was a growing interest in the potential for what the still fairly nascent field of computing could do to hasten this change – progressive change, I should be clear.

Education technology, as I hope my book *Teaching Machines* will eventually make clear, has a history that stretches back into the early twentieth century and has much more in common with Edward Thorndike than it does John Dewey, more in common with multiple choice than with student choice and agency. But in the 1960s and 1970s, we saw progressive education and ed-tech start to coincide. For example, drawing on Seymour Papert's constructionist theories of learning, Daniel Bobrow, Wally Feurzeig, Cynthia Solomon – aha! a woman! – and Papert developed the programming language Logo in 1967, a way for children could to learn computer programming but more importantly even, a way of giving them a powerful object, a powerful tool to think with. And in 1972, along a similar line of thinking, Alan Kay published his manifesto "A Personal Computer for Children of All Ages."

It's perhaps worth reminding you that in the late 1960s and early 1970s, computers were still mostly giant mainframes, and although there was the growing market for microcomputers, these were largely restricted to scientists and the military. Alan Kay was among those instrumental in pushing forward a vision of what we now call "personal computing." Not business computing. Not cryptography. Personal computing.

Kay argued that computers should become commonplace and should be in the hands by non-professional users. He believed this would foster a new literacy, a literacy that would bring about a revolution akin to the changes brought about by the printing press in the 16th and 17th centuries. And key: children would be the primary actors in this transformation.

In "A Personal Computer for Children of All Ages," Kay describes his idea for a device called the DynaBook. He offers his underlying vision for this piece of technology as well as its technical specifications: no larger than a notebook, weighing less than four pounds, connected to a network, and all for a price tag of $500, which Kay explains at length is "not totally outrageous." ($500 was roughly the cost at the time of a color TV, Kay points out.)

"What then is a personal computer?" Kay writes. "One would hope that it would be both a medium for containing and expressing arbitrary symbolic notations, and also a collection of useful tools for manipulating these structures, with ways to add new tools to the repertoire." That is, it would be a computer program but one that is completely programmable by the user – by "children of all ages."

"It is now within the reach of current technology to give all the Beths and their dads a 'DynaBook' to use anytime, anywhere as they may wish," Kay continues. Again, this is 1972 – 40 years before the iPad. "Although it can be used to communicate with others through the 'knowledge utilities' of the future such as a school 'library' (or business information system), we think that a large fraction of its use will involve reflexive communication of the owner with himself through this personal medium, much as paper and notebooks are currently used."

The personal computer isn't "personal" because it's small and portable and sits on your desk at home (not just at work or at school). It's "personal" because you pour yourself into it – your thoughts, your writing, your programming. And as a constructionist framework would tell us, a device like the DynaBook wouldn't be so much about transmitting knowledge to a child but rather it would be about that child building and constructing her own knowledge on her own machine.

Despite looking a lot like today's tablet computer – like an iPad even – Kay insists that his idea for the DynaBook was something very, very different. He told *TIME* magazine last year that the primary purpose of the DynaBook was "to simulate all existing media in an editable/authorable form in a highly portable networked (including wireless) form. The main point was for it to be able to qualitatively extend the notions of 'reading, writing, sharing, publishing, etc. of ideas' literacy to include the 'computer reading, writing, sharing, publishing of ideas' that is the computer's special province. For all media, the original intent was 'symmetric authoring and consuming'."

Consumption versus creation is a tension that's plagued the iPad since it was unveiled, but the DynaBook was designed to handle both at all levels. The hardware, the software, all editable, authorable, tinkerable, hackable, remixable, sharable.

"Isn't it crystal clear," Kay continued, "that this last and most important service [authoring and consuming] is quite lacking in today's computing for the general public? Apple with the iPad and iPhone goes even further and does not allow children to download an Etoy made by another child somewhere in the world. This could not be farther from the original intentions of the entire ARPA-IPTO/PARC community in the '60s and '70s."

For Kay, the DynaBook was meant to help build capacity so that children (so that adults too) would create their own interactive learning tools. The DynaBook was not simply about a new piece of hardware or new software, but again, about a new literacy.

A similar analysis to all this could be made about the programming language Logo. The ed-tech market is now flooded with applications and organizations that promise to teach kids programming. But they aren't Logo pedagogically or philosophically, despite some of them utilizing very cute Turtles in their graphics. Many of these new "learn to code" efforts are about inserting computer science into the pre-existing school curriculum. Computers become yet another subject to study, another skill to be assessed.

In Papert's vision, and in Kay's as well, "the child programs the computer, and in doing so, both acquires a sense of mastery over a piece of the most modern and powerful technology and establishes an intense contact with some of the deepest ideas from science, from mathematics, and from the art of intellectual model building." But as Papert wrote in his 1980 book *Mindstorms*, "In most contemporary educational situations where children come into contact with computers the computer is used to put children through their paces, to provide exercises of an appropriate level of difficulty, to provide feedback, and to dispense information. The computer programming the child."

The computer programming the child.

The computer isn't some self-aware agent here, of course. This is the textbook industry programming the child. This is the testing industry programming the child. This is the technology industry, the education technology industry programming the child.

Despite Kay and Papert's visions for self-directed exploration – powerful ideas and powerful machines and powerful networks – ed-tech hasn't really changed much in schools. Instead, you might argue, it's reinforcing more traditional powerful forces, powerful markets, powerful ideologies. Education technology is used to prop up traditional school practices, ostensibly to make them more efficient (whatever that means). Drill and kill. Flash cards. Now with push notifications and better graphics. Now in your pocket and not just on your desk.

Increasing, education technology works in concert with efforts – in part, demanded by education policies – for more data. We hear these assertions that more data, more analytics will crack open the "black box" of learning. Among those making these claims most loudly – and wildly – is Jose Ferreira, the CEO of Knewton, a company that works with textbook publishers to make content delivery "adaptive." Knewton says that it gathers millions of data points on millions of students each day. Ferreira calls education "the world's most data-mineable industry by far."

"We have five orders of magnitude more data about you than Google has," Ferreira said at a Department of Education "Datapalooza." "We literally have more data about our students than any company has about anybody else about anything, and it's not even close." He adds, "We literally know everything about what you know and how you learn best, everything." (Everything, that is, except the correct usage of the word "literally.")

Education technology has become about control, surveillance, and data extraction. Ivan Illich, Neil Postman, Paulo Freire, Paul Goodman – none of these writers would be surprised to hear that, having already identified these tendencies in the institutions and practices of school.

But to say this – education technology has become about control, surveillance, and data extraction – runs counter to the narrative that computer technologies are liberatory. It runs counter to the narrative that they will open access to information. It runs counter to the narrative that they will simplify sharing. It runs counter to the narrative that they they will flatten hierarchies, flatten the world.

I've heard it suggested quite often that the World Wide Web is an example of what Ivan Illich called "convivial tools" – although his book predates the Web by 15+ years. Illich speaks of "learning webs" in *Deschooling Society*. But I grow less and less certain that the Web is quite what Illich would have meant. But of this, I am certain:

Education technology is not convivial.

Some explanation of what Illich meant by this term, recognizing of course that it's part of his larger critique of modern institutions:

He argued that, "As the power of machines increases, the role of persons more and more decreases to that of mere consumers." In order to build a future society that is not dominated by machines or by industry then, we need to "learn to invert the present deep structure of tools; if we give people tools that guarantee their right to work with high, independent efficiency, thus simultaneously eliminating the need for either slaves or masters and enhancing each person's range of freedom. People need new tools to work with rather than tools that 'work' for them. They need technology to make the most of the energy and imagination each has, rather than more well-programmed energy slaves."

What are convivial tools? They are those that are easy to use. They should be reliable. They should be repairable and durable – and already we can see here how the planned obsolescence of so much of technology veers away from conviviality. Convivial tools should be accessible – free, even. They are non-coercive. They should, according to Illich, support autonomy and agency and enhance the "graceful playfulness" in our social relationships.

"Oh, that sounds like user-centered design!" you might say. Or "that sounds like the free software movement." And again, I have to say: not quite.

The title I gave this talk was "Convivial Tools in an Age of Surveillance." And perhaps that makes it easier to see the challenges in reconciling the conviviality (or lack of conviviality) of user-centered design when we see how technologies are so intertwined now with the power of the state and of industry.

I could have easily chosen a different prepositional phrase. "Convivial Tools in an Age of Big Data." Or "Convivial Tools in an Age of DRM." Or "Convivial Tools in an Age of Venture-Funded Education Technology Startups." Or "Convivial Tools in an Age of Doxxing and Trolls."

It's that last one that's been in my mind a lot lately, particularly in the wake of GamerGate, an ongoing campaign of harassment and threats against women in gaming. It's on my mind, more broadly, because of the culture of the tech sector that claims to be meritocratic but most is assuredly not.

What would convivial ed-tech look like?

The answer can't simply be "like the Web" as the Web is not some sort of safe and open and reliable and accessible and durable place. The answer can't simply be "like the Web" as though the move from institutions to networks magically scrubs away the accumulation of history and power. The answer can't simply be "like the Web" as though posting resources, reference services, peer-matching, and skill exchanges – what Illich identified as the core of his "learning webs" – are sufficient tools in the service of equity, freedom, justice, or hell, learning.

"Like the Web" is perhaps a good place to start, don't get me wrong, particularly if this means students are in control of their own online spaces – its content, its data, its availability, its publicness. "Like the Web" is convivial, or close to it, if students are in control of their privacy, their agency, their networks, their learning. We all need to own our learning –the analog and the digital representations or exhaust from that. Convivial tools would not reduce life to a transaction, reduce our learning to a transaction, reduce our social interactions to a transaction.

I'm not sure the phrase "safe space" is quite the right one to build alternate, progressive education technologies around, although I do think convivial tools do have to be "safe" insofar as we recognize the importance of each other's health and well-being. Safe spaces where vulnerability isn't a weakness for others to exploit. Safe spaces where we are free to explore, but not to the detriment of those around us. As Illich writes, "A convivial society would be the result of social arrangements that guarantee for each member the most ample and free access to the tools of the community and limit this freedom only in favor of another member's equal freedom."

We can't really privilege "safe" as the crux of "convivial" if we want to push our own boundaries when it comes to curiosity, exploration, and learning. There is risk associated with learning. There's fear and failure (although I do hate how those are being fetishized in a lot of education discussions these days, I will say.)

Perhaps what we need to build are more compassionate spaces, so that education technology isn't in the service of surveillance, standardization, assessment, control.

Perhaps we need more brave spaces. Or at least many educators need to be braver in open, public spaces – not brave to promote their own "brands" but brave in standing with their students. Not "protecting them" from education technology or from the open Web but not leaving them alone, and not opening them to exploitation.

Perhaps what we need to build is more consensus-building not consensus-demanding tools. Mike Caulfield gets at this in a recent keynote about "federated education." He argues that "Wiki, as it currently stands, is a consensus *engine*. And while that's great in the later stages of an idea, it can be deadly in those first stages." Caulfield relates the story of the Wikipedia entry on Kate Middleton's wedding dress, which 16 minutes after it was created, "someone – and in this case it probably matters that is was a dude – came and marked the page for deletion as trivial, or as they put it 'A non-notable article incapable of being expanded beyond a stub.'" Debate ensued about the entry's worthiness on its "talk" page, until finally Wikipedia co-founder Jimmy Wales stepped in with his vote: a "strong keep," adding "I hope someone will create lots of articles about lots of famous dresses. I believe that our systemic bias caused by being a predominantly male geek community is worth some reflection in this context."

Caulfield has recently been exploring a different sort of wiki, also created by Ward Cunningham. This one known as the Smallest Federated Wiki – doesn't demand consensus like Wikipedia or other wikis do. Not off the bat at least. Instead, entries – and this can be any sort of text or image or video, it doesn't have to "look like" an encyclopedia – live on federated servers. Instead of everyone collaborating in one space on one server like a "traditional" wiki, the work is distributed. It can be copied and forked. Ideas can be shared and linked; ideas can be co-developed and co-edited. But there isn't one "vote" or one official entry that is necessarily canonical.

Rather than centralized control, we have conviviality. This distinction between Wikipedia and Smallest Federated Wiki hints at something that Illich argued: that we need to be able to identify when our technologies become manipulative. We need "to provide guidelines for detecting the incipient stages of murderous logic in a tool; and to devise tools and tool systems that optimize the balance of life, thereby maximizing liberty for all."

Of course, we also need to recognize – those of us that work in ed-tech and adopt ed-tech and talk about ed-tech and tech writ large – that convivial tools and a convivial society must go hand-in-hand. There isn't any sort of technological fix to make education better. It's a political problem, that is, not a technological one. We cannot come up with technologies that address systematic inequalities – those created by and re-inscribed by education – unless we are willing to confront those inequalities head on. Those radical education writers of the 1960s and 1970s offered powerful diagnoses about what was wrong with schooling. The progressive education technologists of the 1960s and 1970s imagined ways in which ed-tech could work in the service of dismantling some of that drudgery and exploitation.

But where are we now? Instead we find ourselves with technologies working to make that exploitation and centralization of power even more entrenched. There must be alternatives – both within and without technology, both within and without institutions. Those of us who talk and write and teach ed-tech need to be pursuing those things, and not promoting consumption and furthering institutional and industrial control. In Illich's words: "The crisis I have described confronts people with a choice between convivial tools and being crushed by machines."

Sorry. That's the best I can do for a happy ending: remind us that we have to make a choice.

This talk was delivered at New York University on November 13, 2014. The original transcript can be found on Hack Education at http://www.hackeducation.com/2014/11/13/convivial-tools-in-an-age-of-surveillance/

WORKS CITED

Mike Caulfield, "Federated Education: New Directions in Digital

Collaboration." November 6, 2014.
http://hapgood.us/2014/11/06/federated-education-new-directions-in-digital-collaboration/

Jose Ferreira, Knewton at Education Datapalooza.
http://youtu.be/Lr7Z7ysDluQ

Ivan Illich, *Deschooling Society*. Marion Boyars, 1970.

Ivan Illich, *Tools for Conviviality*. Marion Boyars, 1973.

Alan Kay, "A Personal Computer for Children of All Ages." Proceedings of the ACM Annual Conference. 1971. Vol. 1, No. 1.

Seymour Papert, *Mindstorms: Children, Computers, and Powerful Ideas*. Basic Books. 1980.

AFTERWORD

I know the "cool thing" is to sneer at keynotes and lectures. We're supposed to roll our eyes and tut-tut at those who stand up in front of an audience with prepared speeches and PowerPoint presentations. We're supposed to mutter that "nobody really learns that way." It's a short hop from there to the familiar refrain: all educators do is lecture, just like they've been doing for centuries. This is why education hasn't changed in hundreds of years. Blah blah blah.

I'm not prepared to defend keynotes and lectures as the best way to teach or learn. I'm not prepared to defend keynotes and lectures based on the fourteen or so talks I delivered this year. You can read them here and decide their worthiness for yourself. Hopefully, they are thought-provoking. That was the point. I thought and I wrote and I read aloud a lot this year. I've heard people say they didn't really like the delivery but they liked what I said. Duly noted. I'm not an actor. I'm a writer.

I am a writer and I am a learner and I will say this: there are keynotes and lectures that I do listen to again and again. I jot down notes. I hit rewind. I tweet excerpts. I read transcripts. I reread transcripts. I build my own knowledge upon these talks. I recognize that the words, arguments, narratives, sermons, speeches, lectures, essays, elocution have expanded my thinking.

One of those talks that I return to again and again is the closing keynote at NEXT 2013 in Berlin, where science fiction writer Bruce Sterling spoke about "Fantasy Prototypes and the Real Disruption." The theme of the event was "Here Be Dragons." *Hic Sunt Dracones*. It's a phrase that appears in the keynote I delivered at ALT this year (See Chapter 9); it's the phrase that inspired not only "Ed-Tech's Monsters" but this entire book.

In his keynote, Sterling offers what he admits is probably a painful message for an audience of entrepreneurs and designers, an audience the conference itself describes as "digital forethinkers and tech experts": *Those that live by disruption die by disruption.*"

I've written and spoken about disruption a lot over the last few years — not in terms of "design fiction" as Sterling pursues but in terms of folklore, once upon a time my academic discipline. (And perhaps the two are more closely aligned than I'd really ever considered.) I've linked the stories I hear about disruption as I study the history and the business and the politics of ed-tech to Silicon Valley mythology, millennialism, apocalypticism, late capitalism, and End Times fantasies. Sterling links disruption to dragons.

In his keynote at NEXT, Sterling makes it very clear that startup culture lives within the belly of this fiery, disruptive, destructive beast. All this entrepreneurial exuberance is, he argues, actually "a tacit allegiance between the hacker space favelas of the startups and offshore capital and tax avoidance money laundries. And what were they doing? They were building a globalized networked society. And that's what's coming next. An actual globalized networked society."

The globalized networked society that the 1% envisions — the technology investors, the venture capitalists, the banking class — is not progressive or egalitarian or transgressive, despite all the stories that we tell ourselves as we do their bidding, use their products, fatten their wallets. Their globalized networked society is about a finer-tuned surveillance and control, all thanks to the technologies we readily adopt. It's about the extraction of our data, about turning every moment in our lives into some sort of transaction — a transaction for profit and for profiling. Startups tell themselves otherwise, of course. They say they're here to challenge "the system" and "the Man." But "we are all auto-colonialized by the austerity," insists Sterling. "That's your big dragon," he tells them. "That's your actual dragon. ... As long as you are making rich guys richer, you are not disrupting the austerity. You are one of its top facilitators."

These are startups' dragons. These are the technology industry's dragons. These are the dragons of education technology too.

These are our monsters.

I happened to re-watch *Some Kind of Monster* the other night as I was working on the final edits of this book. The 2004 documentary chronicles the heavy metal band Metallica's struggles to record their album *St. Anger.*

I have a strange relationship with the band as *Ride the Lightning* and *Master of Puppets* were soundtracks of my early teen years. But I was never really fan of the band beyond those albums, and I confess, the band's bullshittery around Napster and file-sharing put me solidly in the "I hate Lars Ulrich" camp. Metallica has come to symbolize the vested interests of an industry that purports to be about creativity but that does everything to foreclose creative expression and the enjoyment and sharing of it. Metallica has come to symbolize a resistance to the changes that the Internet will bring about.

There are lessons for education and ed-tech there.

I find *Some Kind of Monster* weirdly fascinating as it offers a pseudo-psychological look into the power struggles between drummer Ulrich and lead singer James Hetfield. That is, it wants to offer a psychological assessment, but it can't, even though the band hired a "performance-enhancing coach" to help them pull themselves together. It wants to make you pick sides in a very old beef among Ulrich and Hetfield and Dave Muscatine and Jason Newsted. But you can't really pick a side. They're all assholes. And the documentary can't really offer you any deep psychological insights either. Even though the filmmakers recognize everyone in Metallica is an asshole (sorry Kirk Hammett — you're an asshole through your complicity) and even though the title suggests there are monsters in Metallica's midst, the documentary only alludes to what it is that makes the band or its members monstrous. It only alludes to psychological or mythological monsters. Fame. Control. Money. Family. Rage. Anger. Alcohol. And in the end, we just shrug and say "that's rock-n-roll."

Metallica still gets to be one of the "Monsters of Rock," despite the vulnerability they supposedly show in the film. Monstrosity remains unexamined. And even more damaging to everyone in the film and in the industry, monstrosity is still demanded and it is still excused, despite the pain and the suffering it causes. Monstrosity is under-theorized in the documentary, even though at some point, the wild success of the band obviously runs counter to its edgy angst.

The filmmakers can't really condemn Metallica as monsters because then they'd face the band's wrath; they'd lose the band's cooperation and permission. So the band is portrayed, with a resigned shrug, as just some kind of monster.

What happens to our monsters? What happens when monsters gain power? What happens to rage when it is recuperated by bigger monsters, by bigger dragons? What happens then to anger? Who do we rage against? Whose rage gets channeled by dragons? By monsters? What gets destroyed in their wake?

I often joke about being called "ed-tech's Cassandra." It's an incredibly serious and incredibly awful name and role to invoke. I already cringe when I'm threatened with violence — with rape and with death. Things didn't work out so well for Cassandra; things didn't work out so well for the Trojans either. I'm not pleased that, by being "ed-tech's Cassandra," I'm placing myself in a familiar tale of destruction and death.

I cannot escape my training as a folklorist. I'm not sure that I would want to. I am fascinated by storytelling. I am fascinated by tradition, by culture, by mythology, by ritual. I recognize that traditions are fragile; culture changes. But I know too that traditions are also incredibly resistant; culture is resilient. It refuses to change.

Humans have long told stories of monsters. Monsters are, quite often, those who live on the edges and the outskirts. Those who defy expectations of appearance and behavior. Monsters transgress. They disobey. They defile. They destroy.

As Cassandra, I must warn you that education technology's monstrosity will bring about our doom. Education technology is the Trojan Horse poised to dismantle public education, to outsource and unbundle and disrupt and destroy. Those who tell you that education technology promises personalization don't actually care about student autonomy or agency. They want surveillance and standardization and control. You have been warned.

Education technology is full of monsters. We've given birth to some of them. We've given birth to the "everyone should learn to code" narrative. We've given birth to the "everyone should be online" story too. We've demanded that everyone have their own device.

Education technology requires our love and our care so as to not become even more monstrous, so that it can become marvelous instead. It demands we resist and we fight and we build and tell a different story. Folks like Seymour Papert started a powerful storytelling for us.

We just need to pick up that tale.

ACKNOWLEDGMENTS

A collection of my public talks, this book would not be possible without those who invited me to speak: the EdTechTeacher iPad Summit, CETIS, the Canadian Network for Innovation in Education, the BC Digital Learning Conference, Berkeley City College, OpenCon, the University of Mary Washington, , the ALT Conference, Pepperdine University, Newcastle University, the Alberta Digital Learning Forum, Emory University, New York University, University of Regina, Justin Reich, Brian Lamb, Martin Hawksey, Sava Saheli Singh, Nicole Allen, George Siemens, Linda Polin, Fabian Banga, Christina Smart, Alec Couros, Katia Hildebrandt, Ryan Brazell, David Morgen, and Suzanne Hardy.

Thank you to everyone who came to hear me speak, who read the original transcripts on Hack Education, who watched the videos and listened to the audio recordings, and who shared my work with others.

And thank you most of all to Kin Lane, who always pushes me and puts up with me and who has helped me optimize my life quite nicely for both happiness and hell-raising. I love you.

IMAGE CREDITS

ABOUT THE AUTHOR

Audrey Watters is a writer who focuses on education technology – the relationship between politics, pedagogy, business, culture, and ed-tech. She has worked in the education field for over 15 years: teaching, researching, organizing, and project-managing. Although she was two chapters into her dissertation (on a topic completely unrelated to ed-tech), she decided to abandon academia, and she now happily fulfills the one job recommended to her by a junior high aptitude test: freelance writer. She has written for *The Atlantic*, *Edutopia*, *MindShift*, *Inside Higher Ed*, *The School Library Journal*, *The Huffington Post*, and elsewhere, in addition to her own blog Hack Education. She is currently working on a book called *Teaching Machines*.